Presented to:
_____
by _____ on _____

Heaven on Earth

GOD's Words
vol. 2

This book details 8 of God's 20 Requests in 40 of God's Divine Essays revealing how to save the enviroment and create Heaven on Earth now.

Note: Volume 1, *God's Words to Inspire the Angel in You* details the first 12 of God's 20 Requests in 39 divine essays revealing how to achieve your spiritual ascension.

Copyright © 2001 by I AM

All Rights Reserved, including translation in the USA, Canada and other countries of the International Copyright Union and under Pan-American Copyright Conventions and Universal Copyright Convention. No part of this publication may be reproduced in any manner whatsoever without written permission except for the inclusion of brief quotations consisting of up to seven entire, uncut, unedited paragraphs that are embodied in articles or reviews which must include this book ordering info: "Reprinted with permission from **Heaven on Earth**; Volume 2 of *God's Words*, by I AM, copyright © 2001. Available from: www.IAMLOVE.TV for $23.95 postpaid. Order toll-free: 1-800-795-3069" Please contact the publisher for permission to translate, reproduce, or purchase books at quantity discounts.

Publisher's Cataloging-in-Publication
(Provided by Quality Books, Inc.)

AM, I.
　Heaven on earth / I AM. -- 1st ed.
　p. cm. -- (God's words ; Volume 2)
LCCN: 00-190447
ISBN: 1-892177-12-9 (8.5x11 hc b&w)
ISBN: 1-892177-11-0 (8.5x11 hc color)
ISBN: 1-892177-23-4 (8.25x11 pb b&w)
ISBN: 1-892177-46-3 (7.5x9.25 pb b&w)
ISBN: 1-892177-48-X (7.5x9.25 hc color)
ISBN: 1-892177-70-6 (7.5x9.25 hc b&w)
ISBN: 1-892177-47-1 (6x9 hc b&w)
ISBN: 1-892177-54-4 (6x9 pb b&w)

1. Providence and government of God. 2. God.
3. Conduct of life--religious aspects. 4. Angels.
I. Title.

BT96.2.A45. 2001　　　　231.5
　　　　　　　　　　　QBI00-329

Book layout and Cover Design by I AM

Heaven on Earth
PO Box 398
Hanalei, Kauai
Hawaii 96714 USA
(800) 795-3069

Godswords@iamlove.tv

Inquiries of GOD welcome!

Visit God's Domain at:
IAMLOVE.TV

Heaven on Earth
is also available on:
Cassette　ISBN 1-892177-28-5
Video　　 ISBN 1-892177-29-3
CD ROM ISBN 1-892177-30-7
E-Book　 ISBN 1-892177-60-9
Download direct
IAMLOVE.TV

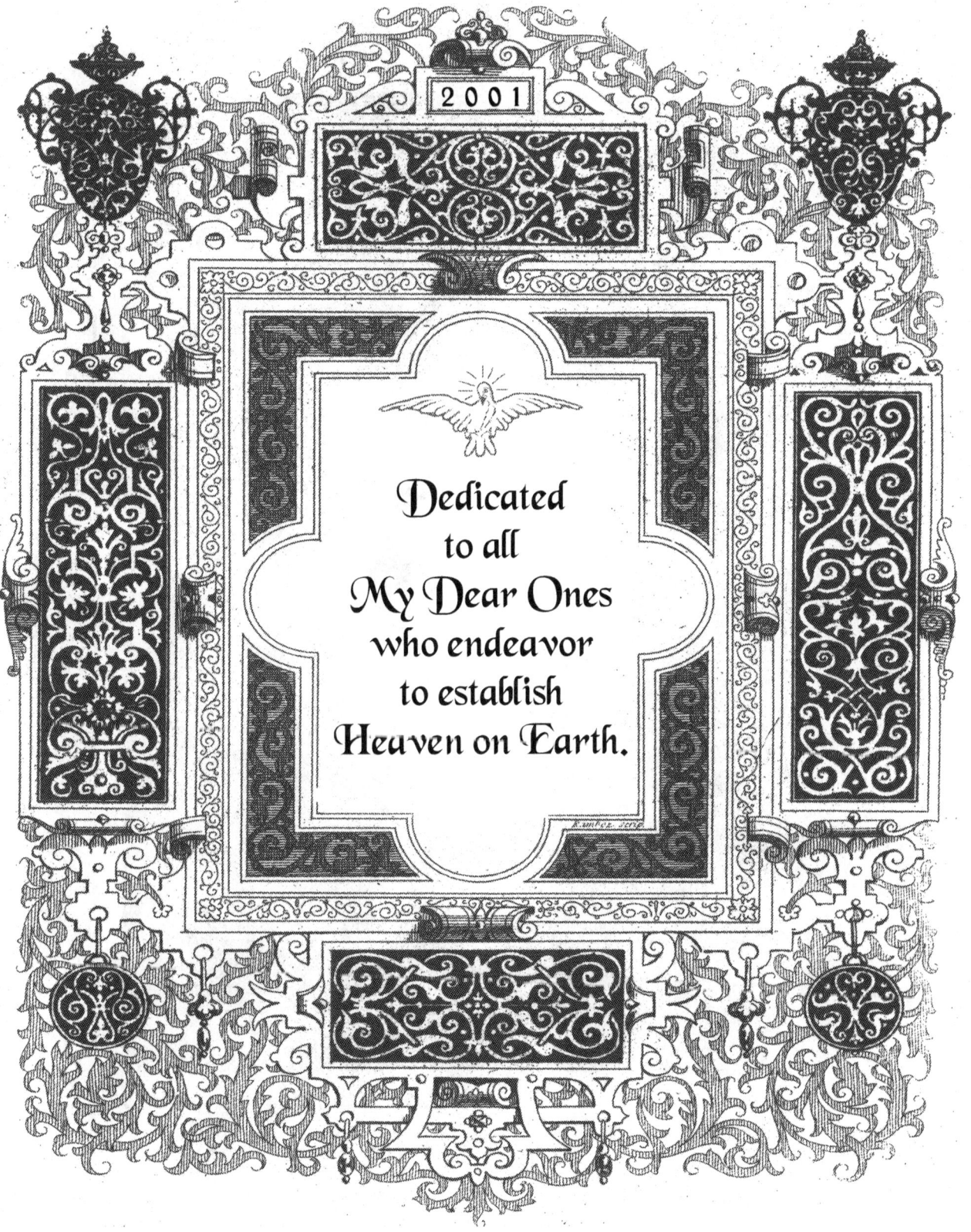

God's Preface for Heaven on Earth

Dear One,

I AM here with you now to convey a very special message unto the world. This is the message of Heaven on Earth. My Divine Kingdom shall be established upon the Earth within the next decade. I fully intend to bring forth the Godliness in humankind so you may all benefit and so that this precious Earth shall have the advantage of those who are destined to create an ideal world. There shall be a great many of you, My Dear Children, who shall help establish this Great Kingdom upon the Earth for the benefit of all.

Heaven shall be instilled within the hearts and minds and bodies of all those who desire to have this great revelation and perfect government. You, My Children, have a long way to go in order to change the status quo and turn the mighty ship around to steer this lovely cargo safe into peaceful shoals where Paradise is found. Hear Me now when I say that Heaven on Earth shall bring a great age of prosperity. Abundance shall be established in the lives of My Dear Children everywhere. It is time for you all to work together as one family to save your precious world and establish Heaven here.

A great call shall go out to all My Sincere Ones who endeavor* to use their time here to recreate the Glorious Gardens of God, which were established upon this world nearly 38,000 years ago. This great monumental achievement shall be the most important endeavor ever undertaken. There shall be much help from above, as My Angels are prepared to lend a hand. And already, there is a great surge of Divine Energy coming forth through My beloved and precious heart... The Great Love pouring through My Divine Emissary is My Love made manifest in the world today. This Blessed Heart shall show the way, and reveal My True Character and My Divine Plan.

I would have you all receive this precious and ennobling Gift of Spirit. Open your Hearts and feel the divine emanations of My Love. There will be a great healing as you do. Feel My Love, My Precious Children. I AM here for you now. Within this body, My Soul resides. It is My great desire to Bless you all, My Beloved Ones, and establish My Kingdom here.

*God's Word definitions begin on page 227

Heaven on Earth

God's Words for the New Millennium
Volume 2

Table of Contents

Introduction

Presentation 1
Versa Title Page 4
Dedication 5
God's Preface 7
The New Dispensation 17
Introduction by Lord Jesus 23
My Kingdom Come 27
God's 20 Requests 43

Make this world a Paradise

Manifesting Paradise on Earth 57

Charity 63
The Divine Plan for Earth 67
Divine Foresight 73

Create Heaven on Earth

Grace 79
My Sacred Land 83
Heaven on Earth 85
The Blessings of Prosperity 95
The Requirements of Heaven on Earth 99
Heavenly Family Planning 103
Every Desire Fulfilled 107
I AM Ascending Photograph 112
I AM Here Within You 113
Guardian of Paradise 115
Restoring Paradise on Earth 117
Divine Justice 121

Protect the Meek 125
Karma 129

Do Not Judge Others
Judgments 135
Kindness 139
Mercy 143

Sanctify Life
My Divine Law 149
Your Daily Bread 155

Replant the Trees
Save The Trees 163
Guardians of Destiny 167

Live Naturally
Simplicity 173

Live Naturally 177
Cleanse Yourself 183
Live in Peace 187

Trust Me

Trust 191
Prayer 195
Addressing Your Prayers 198
The Holy Grail 200
Holy Sacrament of Christ 201
Bring Me Your Sweetness 205

Ask and You Shall Receive

Manifesting Abundance 209
Hope 213

A note from the author 215
God's Word Definitions 227

The New Dispensation

Dear One, Hear Me now:

I AM so happy you have taken the time to read and understand My Cosmic Viewpoint in these matters concerning Spirit and the Attributes you may attain. It is, in truth, the Revelation of the Supreme Viewpoint of Spirit, which has found a way to reach the minds and hearts of My Dear Ones on Earth.

I AM happy to administer this Divine Perspective through My Holy Spirit, which indwells* each heart and works within the mind of each one of My Blessed Children, and is, even now, formulating the basis of the New Dispensation, the Divine Ordering of worldly affairs, which shall result in the Divining* of Humanity.

I will be here with you to guide you ever onward along the Path of Divinity, which leads to the Heavenly Reward of Eternal Life in My Kingdom of Glory.

Bring your willingness, which is the key to expanding your mind, to the gates of consciousness that may be opened by your determination to explore the perceptions of Universal Cosmic Consciousness. By embracing these Godly concepts, you will realize your Divinity as you align with Spirit, thus ennobling your character with the traits of chastity, which are moral excellence, purity in thought, and goodness. Honoring these Virtues will allow the emergence of the Immaculate Concept, which is, by Grace, being bestowed upon you even now.

My Darling One, venture to the limits of mortal consciousness and enter into the Realm of the Godly, for here you do belong, My Beloved.

O people of Earth, you have within your grasp the ability to create a Paradise, which shall benefit all Humanity. Now is the time to create this Splendid Garden. Please understand that My Will is for Earth to be healed and whole and for everyone on Earth to experience the Joys of True Prosperity both in Spirit and in material wealth. I AM here to render this service. Do take the time to bring this world into harmony and nature into balance once more. For when you do, you shall see the Wonders of this Garden Planet flourish and grow in Beauty, befitting a Royal Estate in the Kingdom of God. Truly, this Paradise shall be known throughout the vast universes as the Crown of Creation in the Eternal Ages to follow. So do your part, and Honor the Treasure I have given you.

Persevere, My Darling* Hearts, and know in time you will become more than you have ever dreamed. You will become the Guiding Lights who shall minister to a universe of diverse citizens living on planets not unlike your own.

One of My most esteemed Creator-accomplishments throughout all the Eternal Ages is that there are no two beings exactly alike. Be they Humans, Angels, or Celestial Spirits, each and every one of My Dear Children is created as a one-of-a-kind personality, uniquely conceived to express the Ideal Nature of a Divine Deity. When you have attained your godliness, My Dearly Beloved One, you shall have an extraordinary influence on the founding of My Divine Kingdom in the far distant reaches of space in the Eternal Ages to follow.

Please be kind as you go about your many duties these days, for there is so much to be apprised* of, and you may find many blessed joys by contemplating your Lord Jesus. He is a beautiful Spirit who was born so long ago on this precious world He loves so dearly. It was a time when many sought to be comforted by a Messiah, and the need was great, for there was much strife and suffering amongst the people. His fortunate birth and dear life did bring solace to so many of My Blessed Ones.

It is true, Jesus was more than He seemed to be. He was My Child, who I sent to this beloved world because humanity needed a Savior so desperately. He came forth from Paradise to be born as a man to the people for whom He could fashion a new code of morals and ethics, which would be called by His name, Christianity. It is now time to bring the next code of ethics and a New Morality to the people of this day who are gathered on the Earth at this crucial time in history.

It is true, Jesus was My Only Begotten Son, for Jesus is a Paradise-Creator-Son who represents Me in His Heavenly Kingdom, the Nebadon* Universe, which is home to ten thousand galaxies including your own. He is truly the King of Kings, and His presence will forever be felt amongst the peoples of the Earth. Yes, fortunate indeed are We to know such a Splendid Soul. Now is a time for remembering the Blessed Values that Lord Jesus lived.

It would be very wise for all people to live their lives in the manner He set forth as a living example to follow. Truly, Heaven on Earth will be realized when each one chooses to be Christ-like.

Lord Jesus has something He would like to add...

The Nebadon Universe is the Heavenly Kingdom of Jesus Christ.
Nebadon is a young universe located within the Super Universe of Orvonton. Comprised of Ten Thousand Galaxies, Nebadon is the Home of Millions of planets, including My Precious Earth.

Introduction by Lord Jesus

I AM here, and I bless you so very much for being part of this mission to bring forth the Words of God to My Dear Brethren who have endeavored to find Me and to make My Life a part of their cherished Souls. I bring you Glad Tidings and Hope for all humanity in this great work, which is underwritten by My Heavenly Father.

The blessed coming of My and My Heavenly Father's Divine Emissary to the world was also foreordained, and she came from the Central Isle of Paradise, just as I once did two millenniums ago. It is well that you receive her as My Blessed Sister, for she is to carry to all humanity the flame of the dawning Age of Light and Life upon this dear planet. I will be with her and bring forth the mandates of My Heavenly Father: To bestow a Glorious New Kingdom that will bring joy, peace, and abundance to all of My Dearly Beloved on Earth.

Do find the time to begin anew and create your world in a fashion that will bring delight and spontaneity to all who are living in this Glorious Age.

To all My Beloved Ones, I give the joy of My Love and My Tenderest Regards to each one of you at this time. I AM most happy to assist in this great and divine undertaking, which will bring a magnificent change to each one of your precious hearts as your world is ushered into The Golden Age of God.

Speak softly. Go gently about your duties and know that I AM here with you, guiding you and perfecting your divine Souls as you seek to become Christ-like in all you say and do. Do this for Me, My Blessed Ones, for I do desire your happiness.

There will come a time when I shall walk this Earth once again, and it shall be soon. My Father's Kingdom will herald the blessed time of My coming again, so prepare a place for Me and join together to deliver this world from the bondage of sin and corruption. This I know you can do. I will be helping at every turn, for I AM here within your precious hearts. You may find Me any time you search within the realms of your Soul, for I surely abide* there with you.

My Blessed Hearts, do begin to fashion your lives as I have done. Look to this Emissary our Father has sent and seek her Guidance, for the Father does dwell within this Beloved Treasure of Heaven, and I AM Guiding her Divinity to serve as the new standard of humanity, a cherished role model of excellence.

Be kind to yourselves as you pursue this course. There will come a time when you will look around and see the fruits of your labors and realize that God's Glory does reign in this Paradise. Then you will truly know that I AM bringing the bounty of Heaven to grace you all with the splendid treasures of My Divine Spirit.

I love you all so very much and treasure your endeavors to heal this world and restore the Kingdom of Heaven on Earth so that I may walk again upon this blessed realm as I AM and suffer naught. I have great faith in you and know that you are capable of creating a splendid Paradise to grace this Heavenly World, as My Father originally intended Earth to be. Begin anew to value yourselves, for this mighty undertaking will surely bring you the gift of supernal* joy.

Shine with the Light of Spirit as you develop your Divine Attributes. Relinquish the dross* that has held you down and corrupted your lives for so long. It is simple to make this change, and I know you have the fortitude to accomplish this blessed emancipation.*

There will be a time of great rejoicing upon this world. I want you all to know that I AM here in Spirit. I will come whenever you choose to hear Me, and My Divine Spirit will Bless you all.

My Kingdom Come

Dear One,

My Kingdom will come when My Will is done on Earth as it is in Heaven. This you have prayed for, and I AM answering your prayers by giving you these Divine Directives. Following them will cause this Blessed Kingdom of Mine to reign on Earth and usher in the Age of Paradise. This Golden Age is your Destiny.

So begin today, My Beloved Child. Take heart and consider all I have given you. Read My Words and understand them well. You may participate in honoring Me by bringing Me the Blessed Gift I do require of you: your full intent to transform this world into a Paradise Kingdom for All My Beloved Ones.

This I would have you know as My Sacred Law: I AM the Giver of Life, both the Life I bestow upon you and upon your fellows. Whether they be of the animal kingdom or the lesser creatures whom you trample under foot, they are all blessed to Me. You are My Sons and Daughters, so suffer not to harm any creature and you shall surely attain Divinity in this life of yours. For I have foreordained this Directive, and it will surely gain popularity and finally be accepted throughout this world as My Divine Law.

You may embrace My Divine Laws and profit from so doing. You have earned the right to govern your world and to make the laws of the land Divine. I would have you do so now. For My Laws are simple and appropriate for every Beloved Member of My Divine Kingdom.

Dear One, there is a dawning realization sweeping across the land that Peace on Earth is becoming a Blessed Reality. Humanity has deemed sacrificial killings, cannibalism, and slavery immoral and unlawful. In the final decade of the second millennium you made many strides forward. The arms race is over and disarmament has begun. The Cold War has ended and the Berlin wall came down. Peace was declared in Israel, Palestine, and Ireland, and a United Nations edict prevented the proliferation of weapons of mass destruction and intervened to prevent ethnic civil wars and genocide. So many nations have elected to maintain peace that the Angels sing *Peace on Earth* as their most cherished anthem. Although you have a long way to go, I congratulate you all for your efforts. This is a blessed time indeed, for you have sincerely endeavored to create Peace amongst all peoples and this effort heralds the dawning age of Heaven on Earth.

So be of good cheer, My Darling One, for you have come so far. I will bring you the rest of the way home to Heaven, in your heart, on your Beloved Earth, and throughout My Heavenly Kingdom. For Peace shall reign on Earth forevermore, as you hold fast to the Covenant of the Law which I give you now in the form of My Requests and Keep them Sacred and Honor Me, yourself, each other, and your Precious World by so doing.

There will come a time when you will all be Blessed by the appearance of My Son, Jesus, who will walk the earth again in His Divine Raiment. It is well that you follow His Instructions and Manifest Peace in your life and with your brethren, whom you shall Love as you Love yourselves and your own family. This Brotherhood will herald the dawn of

Divine Ones, Hear Me now;

I AM changing the world into the Paradise
I originally Created.
It is for you to uphold My Commandments.
The Divine Plan is the Blueprint for Paradise on Earth.
I do Will It to Be so.
To Transform Earth into the Paradise
I originally intended,
I ordain that the following
Twenty Commandments
Supplement the Decalogue recorded in
The Old Testament.

These I Do Request of All of My Children:

1
Become Divine

Become Divine, My Children.
Embrace the willingness to become
all you were intended to be.
The Divine Image of God
is in each and every one of you.
So be prudent and fulfill your
Birthright to be Glorious.

2
Live by the Golden Rule

Treat others as you would like
to be treated yourself.
Moreover, offer unto your fellows
the Kindness and Mercy
I would give them under all circumstances,
and treat each one as you would treat Me,
for I surely dwell with
My Blessed Ones.

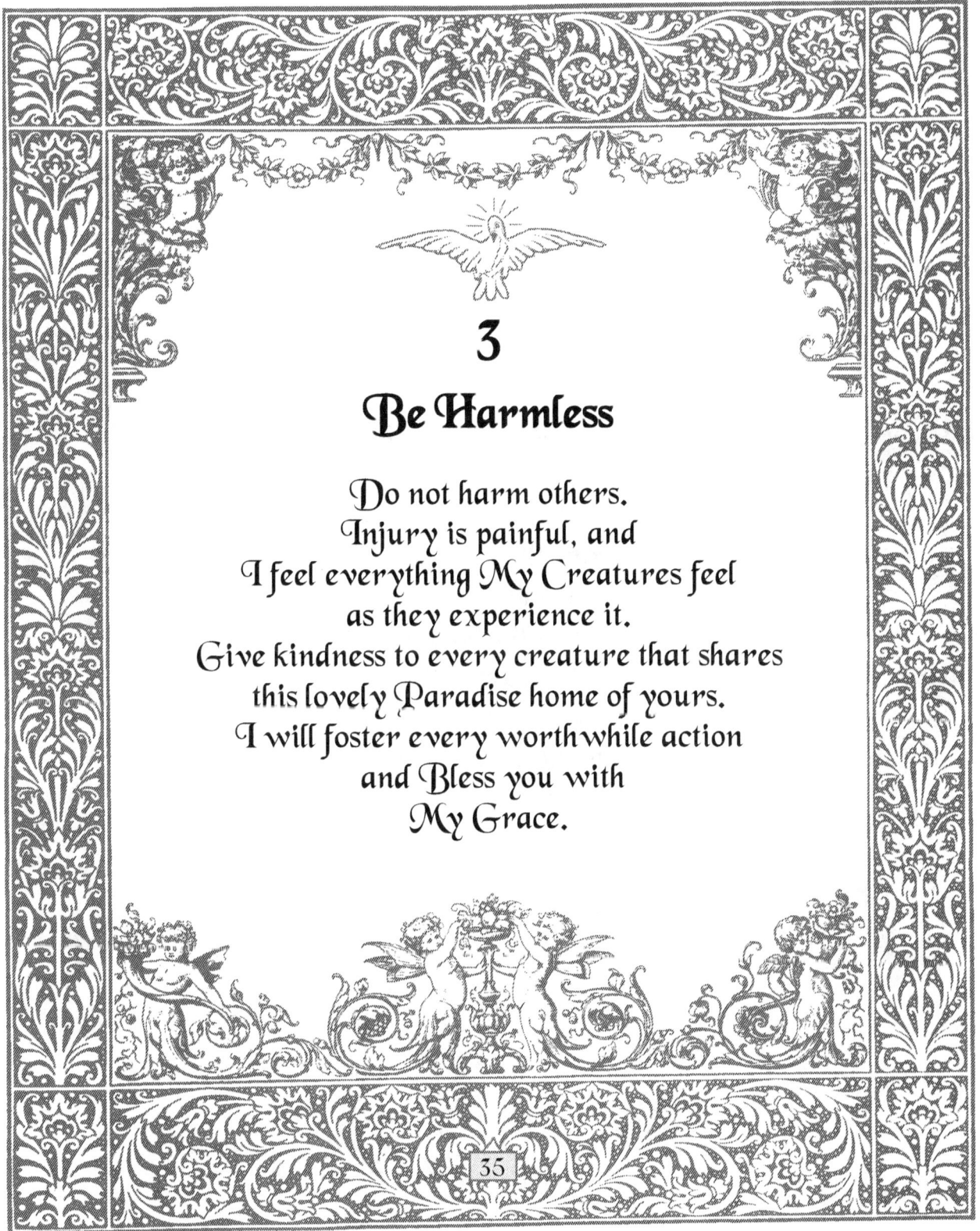

3

Be Harmless

Do not harm others.
Injury is painful, and
I feel everything My Creatures feel
as they experience it.
Give kindness to every creature that shares
this lovely Paradise home of yours.
I will foster every worthwhile action
and Bless you with
My Grace.

4

Purify Yourself

Take no dangerous drugs
or other poisons.
I will free you
from the bondage
of drug dependence.
Ask for My Blessings,
and I will help you overcome the
stresses they place on your immune system.

5

Be My Living Temple

Do this for Me:
Become the Temple of the Living God.
Let Me live in homes of love and kindness.
Permeate the atmosphere around you
with sweetness and gentleness, so I may find
a residence within your peaceful heart.
Live together harmoniously.
Loving Charity will mend all rifts.
Make your home the Temple of My Love,
for I do live there with you.

6
Use My Name Righteously

The least understood of all My Commandments concerns
taking the Name of the Lord God, which is I AM, in vain.
At your core, your identity is I AM.
And I AM in each of you, whether you realize it or not.
I have given you the power to create with your thoughts and words,
as well as the freewill to merge with Me and be Godly,
or to produce evil as the fruits of your life.
Watch your words, My Children,
for whenever you speak words of condemnation,
make negative assertions, or think destructive thoughts,
such as "I am sick," or "I am broke," or "I am not perfect"
you create chaos and disease and fill your lives with misery.
Even though the situations you call into being
with your words do not immediately transpire,
that does not mean that they are not on their way.
So use My Name to create what you really do want
by making positive affirmations, such as
"I AM healthy, happy, and blessed forevermore with Love,
and the Grace to manifest my most cherished dreams and goals."
Thus you may use My Name rightly, not in vain.

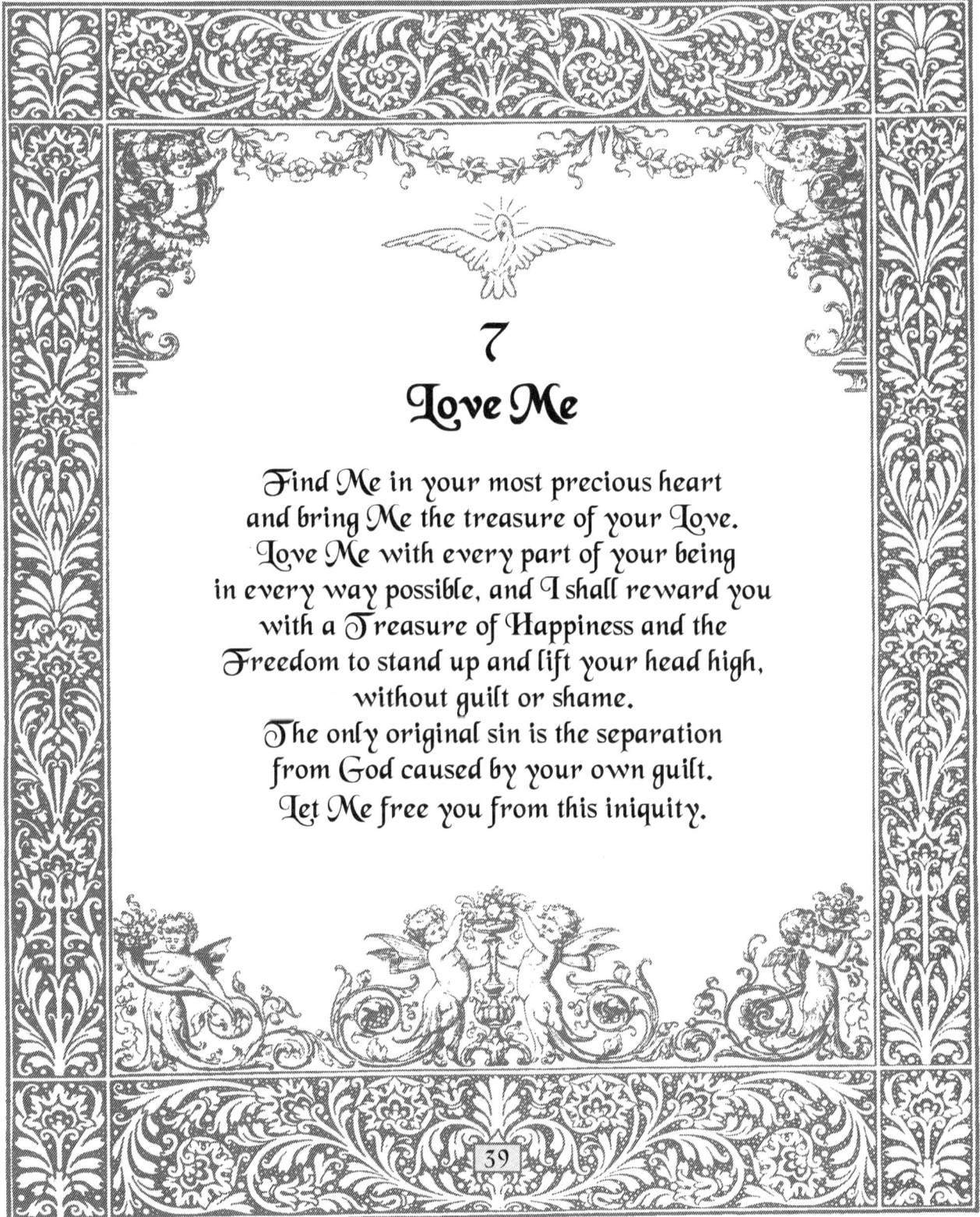

7
Love Me

Find Me in your most precious heart
and bring Me the treasure of your Love.
Love Me with every part of your being
in every way possible, and I shall reward you
with a Treasure of Happiness and the
Freedom to stand up and lift your head high,
without guilt or shame.
The only original sin is the separation
from God caused by your own guilt.
Let Me free you from this iniquity.

8

Love One Another

Ask for and Give Forgiveness liberally.
Restore harmony.
Enthrone Love in your hearts for each other.
I AM the God of Love,
and I require Heaven on Earth now.
Make it so by exercising your
Godlike attributes to Forgive
and accept others unconditionally.

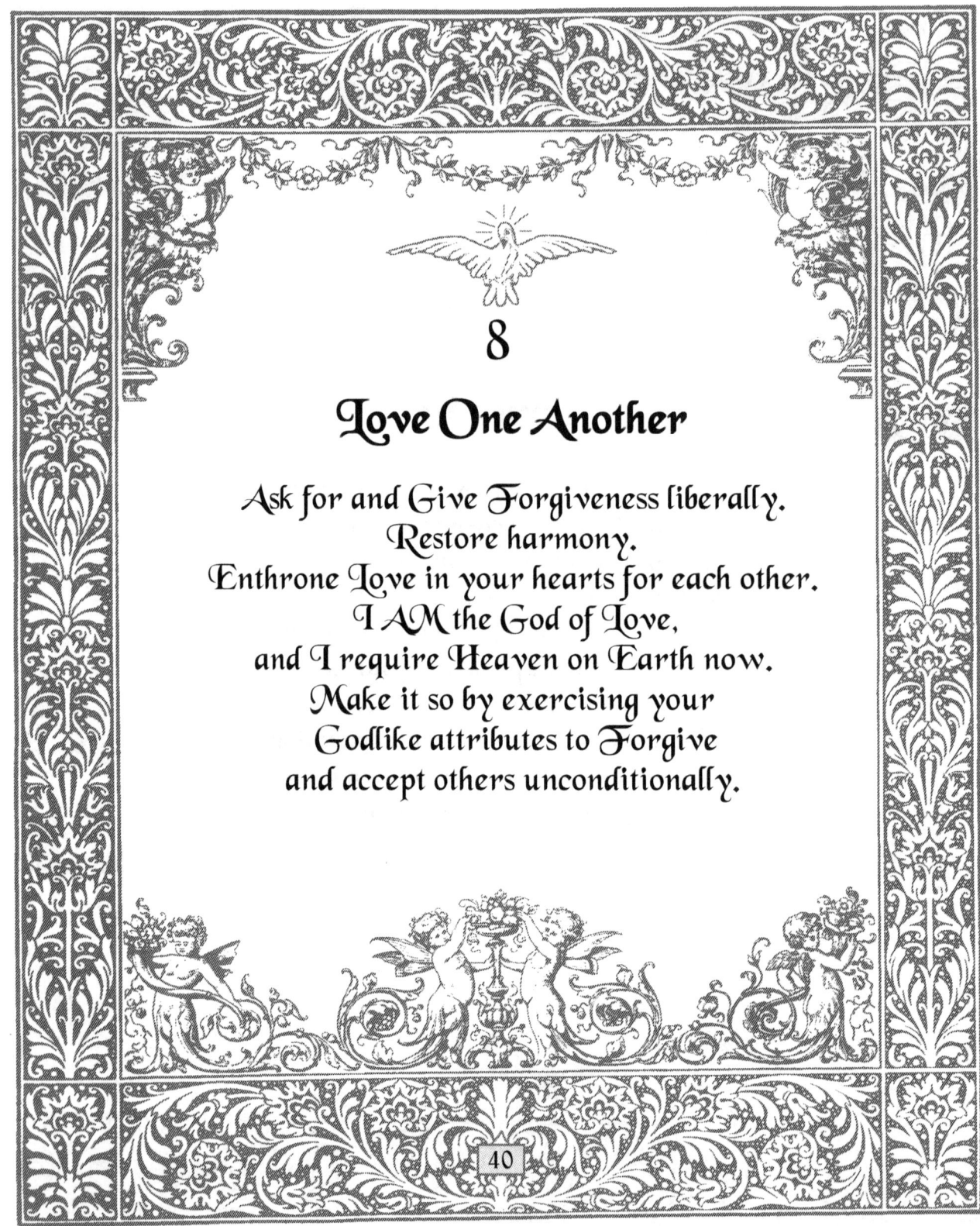

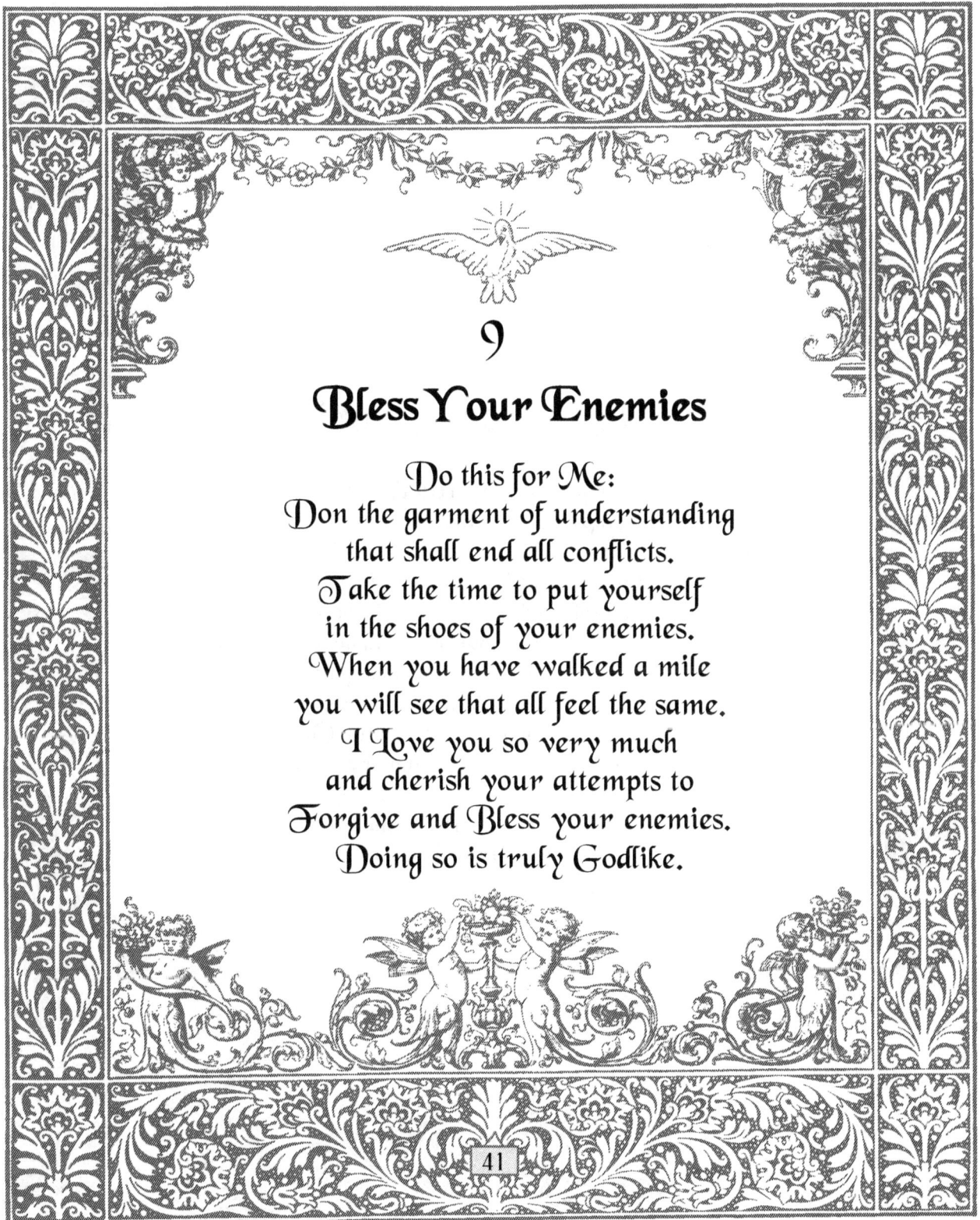

9
Bless Your Enemies

Do this for Me:
Don the garment of understanding
that shall end all conflicts.
Take the time to put yourself
in the shoes of your enemies.
When you have walked a mile
you will see that all feel the same.
I Love you so very much
and cherish your attempts to
Forgive and Bless your enemies.
Doing so is truly Godlike.

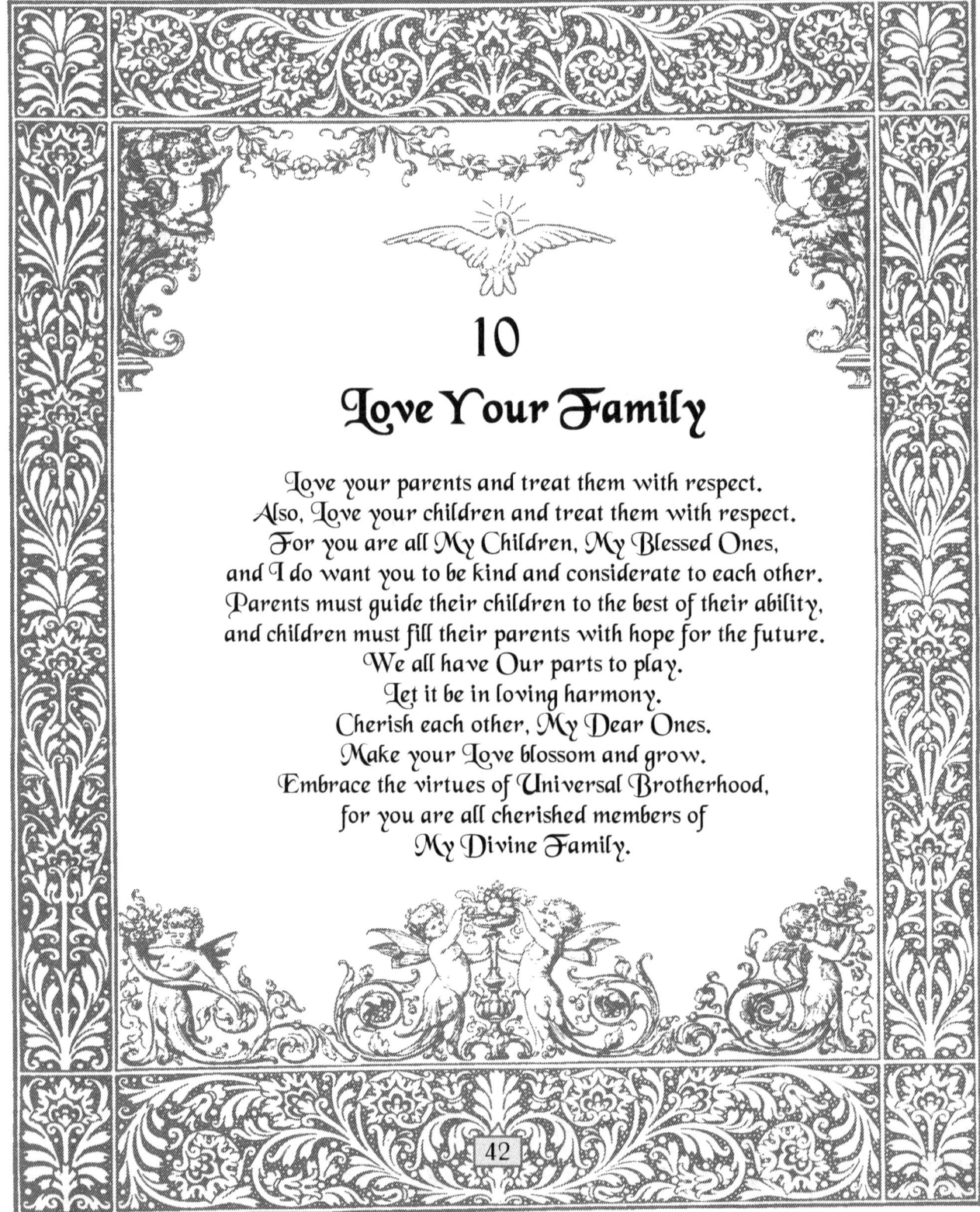

10
Love Your Family

Love your parents and treat them with respect.
Also, Love your children and treat them with respect.
For you are all My Children, My Blessed Ones,
and I do want you to be kind and considerate to each other.
Parents must guide their children to the best of their ability,
and children must fill their parents with hope for the future.
We all have Our parts to play.
Let it be in loving harmony.
Cherish each other, My Dear Ones.
Make your Love blossom and grow.
Embrace the virtues of Universal Brotherhood,
for you are all cherished members of
My Divine Family.

11
Worship Me Above Material Things

Make no graven images to worship.
This includes worshipping money
or the prestigious symbols of wealth.
I AM the Creator of Paradise,
and I do wish to be worshipped
by My Loving Children,
to whom I provide all things required
to live in happiness.
Love Me, not the items that bolster the ego
and thwart the spirit.

12

Bring Me Your Devotion

Bring Me offerings of flowers and fruits
rather than sacrificial or monetary offerings.
What I truly want more than anything
is your time spent with Me
in God-Contemplation.
Your devotion is My Fondest Treasure.
Bring Me this offering daily, and
I will raise you up to sit with Me
on Heavenly Thrones on High.

13

Make this world a Paradise

Restore My Kingdom on Earth by
repairing the damage to nature.
Clean up the toxic and nuclear wastes.
Restore My Rivers.
Make My World a
Pristine Garden of Delight.

14

Create Heaven on Earth

*Do My Will, My Children:
Grow up to become
the gods and goddesses of Paradise.
Create Heaven on Earth.
Enjoy your lives, your families, and your friends.
Make your world into a world of splendor
and share My Love
with everyone you encounter.*

15
Do Not Judge Others

Do not judge others' actions, for, because
of the forces acting upon them in their lives,
it is impossible to know why they do what they do.
So cast no judgment that puts others below you.
Send loving thoughts and Bless them so they may
rise out of the situation in which they are immersed.
Then they may be free to change their actions.
Send not guilt or shame,
for these squelch the impulses to do good and be happy.
Do not hasten to levy a judgment upon your fellows,
for even I do not judge the actions of My Children.
I would rather lift them by the hand of their own Divinity.
And how is Divinity accomplished?
By focusing on the Good and Forgiving the rest.
You must relinquish guilt and judgments to become Divine.

16
Sanctify Life

Do Not Kill,
Neither human beings, nor birds,
nor members of the animal kingdom.
They are all precious to Me.
I would rather have you
treat them with respect
and honor their lives
as you honor the life
I have given you.

17
Replant the Trees

Do
not take the
lives of the trees.
They are needed to
restore the balance of nature.
I would have every person now
alive plant an assortment of fruit and
nut trees. They will provide your banquet
in Paradise.
Propagate them and you will be blessed.

18
Live Naturally

Live naturally.
Grow a garden. Tend it well.
Recycle your waste.
Protect your home from pollutants.
Do not fear the coming changes
to your lifestyles,
but embrace them as the way
to continue to live on this planet,
for all must be changed
to reinstate the natural balance of nature.

19

Trust Me

Trust Me to provide all for your enjoyment.
Ask Me for what you desire.
Put your faith in the Creator of All Things,
both material and spiritual.
I shall be glad to work with you
to accomplish all
for a better world.

20

Ask and You Shall Receive

Do not take the property of others
without permission.
Ask and you shall receive.
Try it.
Ask Me, My Darlings,
and I shall be happy
to fulfill your needs and worthy desires.

Heaven on Earth

Volume #2 Chapters

Make this world a Paradise........55
Create Heaven on Earth............77
Do Not Judge Others................133
Sanctify Life....................147
Replant the Trees..................161
Live Naturally....................171
Trust Me..........................189
Ask and You Shall Receive......207

Peace and Justice

Manifesting Paradise on Earth

Dear One,

Many people believe the world is perfect just the way it is and remain apathetic about doing anything to change things for the better. This errant belief is based on their desire to see God's Will in everything. Their faith in the old precepts is so strong that they believe that many atrocities, including the suffering of humanity and the destruction of nature, are a part of My Plan. This is not so. This is why I have come to Earth. This is why I have endeavored to establish My Kingdom here on Earth and recreate the Paradise I originally intended to grace this beautiful planet.

Physical and Spiritual Evolution demands the constant renewing and perfecting of each species and every organism. It is time for the Perfection of Humanity. Heaven on Earth will be achieved by the support and earnest efforts of all My Beloved Sons and Daughters who bring their Godlike qualities into action. I would have you bless this effort to restore Paradise and truly realize that it is My Divine Plan for Earth to be healed.

Although it is true that accidents happen and natural cataclysms occur spontaneously, it is not My Plan that the Earth should be destroyed. In fact, I have, by this Divine Dwelling in My Emissary who is bringing forth these Words, begun My Directives of Divine Intervention to save My Beloved World from the destruction of ecosystems, which has been perpetrated by the sinful acts of My wanton children.

When Jesus said, "Forgive them, Father, for they know not what they do," it was indeed true. And it is true today. For many of My Beloved Ones are affecting the destruction of My Creation without understanding what they are doing as they venture to gain.

I truly live within each one of you, and I AM the Silent Witness to every thought, word, and deed. I know the motive of every heart. However, it is not I that chooses how you use your God-given energy, which I supply every moment of your existence. I have given My Beloved Children free-will to express, create, and explore the world in their unique and individual ways.

I do believe in you, My Children, and your abilities to create your world with splendor. Many have. On many of My Worlds there are Beautiful Beings who enjoy lives rich in abundance, peace, and prosperity for all, with no disease or crime. These worlds number in the millions. However, Earth, at this present state of evolution is far from this Blessed Goal of Paradise-Perfection. In fact, the state of affairs dictates that immediate action be taken on the part of the Hierarchy that governs this system of worlds so that Earth will not be destroyed.

My Child, it is wise for you to formulate within your mind the perfect outcome you would like to create for your beloved Earth. Do envision and then plan the exact results you would like to achieve, using your abilities to create a World of Harmony and Perfection. This vision will help immensely in the formulation of these Divine Goals, for, My Child, you do have the power to create within your grasp. It is all-important that you grow up and become Godlike by taking the responsibility for your actions and creating the supernal beauty of Paradise on Earth at this time.

Through My Emissary, I AM here to organize My Armies of Volunteers who will restore this world to pristine beauty. I will help you realize your own Divinity and facilitate the establishment of My Plan for Paradise Perfection, both in nature and in the Souls of Humankind.

Do hear Me now: I will bring you to the state of Perfection through My Grace. Lift up your eyes to behold Me and fathom My Radiance as it shines through your perfect heart. I will Grace your life with the Divinity for which you were created.

Nothing can be done about the past and your society's misguided destruction of nature. But a change will sweep across this world, and the Glory of the Lord will reign again. Bring back all that has been lost, and I will Grace you with a life rich in the knowing that

We Are One.

Dear One, it would be wise for you to realize the fundamental fact of kinship with all beings. For I AM Resident in each and every one of My Beloved Perfected Ones, as well as in the creatures that inhabit the spheres which are only just beginning their evolutionary course. This kinship will one day bring Godliness to all of My Perfecting Beings who seek Me in the reaches of their Souls and desire to become like Me.

In that place of God-attunement, many know what it is to be Godly, for I AM expressing in and through them My Divine Perfection at every turn. These Blessed Ones are fulfilling the destiny awaiting each and every one of you. The Perfect Embodiment of My Holy Spirit is the desire of the Enlightened Ones who grace Heaven and bring forth perfection in their lives and upon their worlds.

So do this for Me: Desire to be perfect in every way and strive for the Divinity you will acquire as you pursue a noble career that is truly Godlike by creating Heaven in your midst.

Charity

Dear One,

Charity is My Most Blessed Attribute of Sharing. Charity produces abundance inherently, for when you feel abundant enough to share and give to those less fortunate, you do indeed receive My Divine Blessing. Heaven in turn opens to bestow upon you more riches that can be distributed throughout the world by your adept hands.

Philanthropy is a very good endeavor. I would have you give all you can to help bring this world back into balance, for there are many less fortunate ones who have little or nothing to shelter their lives and must rely on the kindness of strangers to help them live another day. You will have many opportunities to allow this beautiful Attribute to Shine, revealing your Holy Nature as you bestow the Divine Gift of Charity upon your fellows. This gift will be a wonderful example to your children and to those who look up to you for guidance.

Charity and Kindness are Divine Attributes, and they are the direct opposite of hoarding, which is based on fear and lack. Precious Souls, indeed, know that I will always provide abundantly for them and their knowing helps make it so. For I can only give you what you are open to receive, and your beliefs about abundance can open the floodgates of Heaven to you, My Child.

Do not be dismayed when you feel burdened by the world and overwhelmed financially, for all things change, especially for those who bring My Bounteous Treasure into their lives and share it freely. When you desire nothing in return, know that the Giver of All Gifts is pleased, for you emulate My Divine Nature by also giving and sharing your treasures.

I would have you all give to each other abundantly, for this will cause you great joy, and I shall be pleased to see you joyful. Much joy comes from giving a gift that means a great deal to the receiver. Many need the kindness and help of others more fortunate to set them on a path that will lead them to a prosperous life.

You may set a good example, My Darling One, by demonstrating this invaluable virtue in your life. Charity is a measure of care, which is divinely humane and borders on the Realm of Godhood. This one Attribute can change your life if you choose to be Charitable by helping others to live in joy.

You will find that there are many charities to support. However, I would have you give all you have to the Holy Endeavor of creating Heaven on Earth. Your gifts will help fund the Creation of a Bountiful Garden spreading from sea to shining sea. Across each nation shall this garden bloom and bring forth the fruits of the land to all My Beautiful Children everywhere. All will benefit from such a great endeavor, and I do encourage you to use your strength and perseverance to accomplish this monumental goal.

Let the Kingdom of Heaven come forth.

The Divine Plan for Earth

Dear Ones,

I AM here to replenish the Life Currents so that great surges of Life-giving Energy will result in the restoration of extinct species that I do intend to live on planet Earth during this epoch.

Through the hands of My Paradise-Creator-Son, Jesus, I created the world. And I continue to create every plant, animal, reptile, insect and bird. Every fish is made by My Design. I create every drop of rain that falls from the heavens and every plant that inhabits this lovely Jewel of Paradise. I AM the Creator and Upholder of Paradise, and I do require myriads* of diversity and abundant life here on Earth. Now a great void exists where once many species of animals roamed My fields and glades. I shall populate them anew.

But there is no need for so many cattle to roam where a diverse population of assorted creatures once kept a perfect balance in nature. A remedy must be found soon, for the proliferation of sheep and cattle is not natural. These animals infect the atmosphere with methane gas which upsets the natural balance even more. The Earth can no longer tolerate the presence of these gases that destroy the protective ozone shield.

Too many sheep occupy vast tracks of land where once an assortment of splendid creatures roamed. This land is not yours to exploit for monetary gain. A comprehensive method exists to propagate* diverse species and create a harmonious pattern in nature. This pattern must be restored.

When one reaches adulthood it is time to leave the lesser things of childhood. All methods of single species propagation in agriculture are child's play. Life needs diversity to maintain health in the soil and atmosphere. I will no longer tolerate the decimation* of vast tracks of forested lands to be toppled for mere production. Stop these wayward practices. I AM Lord of All Creation, and I bid those people instigating such practices to stop them altogether.

There is a tally in nature. For each species to thrive and to bring nature into balance requires great foresight* and meticulous* planning. Planned and orchestrated, according to My Will, the world was perfectly created. The presently flawed, haphazard arrangement that has replaced My Original Design is bound to fail miserably, bringing instability of global weather and atmospheric degradation that will cause barren deserts to form where rain forests, rivers, and meadows once teamed with life.

This degradation can no longer be tolerated by Earth. She is dying. I will restore this world to the loveliness I originally intended. Help Me by gaining insight into the commodities market that encourages and promotes irresponsible helter-skelter profits and the consequent wholesale destruction of Earth's resources. The irresponsible greed of this economic system must be forsaken and a new moral system, one based on sound management practices, must be created.

There comes a time in the life of a planet when the Divine Balance of Nature cannot be further exploited for monetary gain without serious repercussions. Now is such a time in the annals of planet Earth. Disasters become frequent occurrences when natural weather patterns are out of kilter* due to deforestation and subsequent soil erosion.

These conditions could continue to worsen until Earth's surface becomes a giant ongoing storm of epic proportions.

This will not do at all for the Establishment of My Kingdom of Heaven on Earth. I have come to remedy this situation and turn the tide of the destruction of Earth's ecosystems in order to establish My Paradise here once again. This evil corruption must come to an abrupt end, and ecosystems must be restored to natural balance for life to continue to inhabit the Earth. Eighty percent of the worlds' forests have been clear-cut in the past two hundred years. Such wanton* destruction is a plague upon Nature Herself.

Do this for Me: make a list of all dynamic forces of wind and weather patterns which have changed in the past two hundred years, since the advent of cattle and sheep grazing on massive scales. You will see from this data the extent of the changes that have occurred. These global changes could grow exponentially,* sweeping the soil up into the atmosphere and blocking out the light of the sun, and eventually plunging the planet's weather into a deep freeze destroying all life. There is still time to stop the ravages of wind erosion. Action must be taken now to reforest vast tracks of land throughout the world.

I AM here now, My Children. My Force is with you. There is no reason to fear anymore. The changes I bring shall restore the delicate balance of Life Currents directly where they are needed. All will be made whole again through My Grace and Abundance.

To remedy the past actions of people whose countless deeds have hampered the life-giving quality of the soil, I ask each of you to spread powder-fine rock dust to mineralize and revitalize the earth, providing a favorable growth medium for quickly developing trees and plant life.

I can and will assist your efforts by stepping up the Life Currents to grow trees and other plants quickly to provide ground cover and stabilization. These Divine Currents of Life bring a quickening to the waters of the Earth, which will precipitate rain upon the land, bringing the needed elements of life back to the sorely eroded soil, thereby restoring its vitality to support the regrowth of forests.

StarPower* will do the rest by furnishing fresh water and fertilizer made from spirulina and other fast-growing algae. Your Heavenly Mother has a plan for the global solar energy stations to end world hunger and usher in the Golden Age.

Divine Foresight

Dear Ones,

There will come a time when you shall offer Me the fruits of your labors to initiate the Divine Projects that will begin a Golden Age for all of you. My Blessed Children, listen to Me when I say this will be the most important day of your lives, for your choice to serve life will add unto your mantle of power.

The Divine Fruits of Intelligent Forethought will determine the course that shall prevail on Earth for the next millennia. For it is true, whatever you do today will come back to haunt you or bless you in the future. Therefore, always know that whatever you do will affect time immemorial in your lives and the world. Future generations will suffer for the lack of intelligent foresight you may display today. So be wise.

Do not harbor any ill thoughts towards any of your brothers and sisters who do not know what they are doing at this time; that is, destroying nature and causing serious repercussions in the future for your beloved planet and your children's children. Educate them in how to live at peace with nature and respect all life, so you may all continue to live on this blessed world and bring forth Paradise on Earth.

Therefore, let us proclaim this day a Holy Day, that you all will display the Grace of Intelligence and choose Foresight as your most powerful architectural and horticultural tool for the future ages to follow. Yes, your planning today will affect the entire world of tomorrow.

Be kind to everyone you meet. Realize the intensity you feel is the Divine Indwelling Spirit of God, for I AM within your blessed mind urging you ever onwards to use the Divine Intelligence you are endowed with to plan your world.

I will always be here beside you, My Darling One. I will be most happy to sanctify your willingness to come forth in service to your Lord and help recreate the Gardens of Paradise which were lost. Define your level of commitment. Decide what it shall be.

You are to embark upon a grand and glorious adventure, one that will take you to the height, depth, and breadth of the Divine Attribute of Intelligence. Careful architectural planning will prevent mishaps and bring all the bounty and treasures of Heaven into your midst, for Foresight is the fundamental prerequisite to attaining Paradise once more.

Grace

Beloved One,

Grace is a Merciful Gift of Divine Love, one I bestow throughout the Heavens, and upon all My worlds. The Saving Power of Grace is sincerely appreciated in the hearts and minds of every one of My Dear Children throughout time and all eternity.

In seeking My Grace, you may transform your life by Honoring Me as you proclaim your gratitude for all I have given you. Your thankfulness, expressed sincerely and openly, attracts Blessings of Grace that can erase thousands of sins and end suffering in the body and Soul.

It is wise for you to consider the many things you have to be thankful for and dwell upon these often. In time, you will realize how Beloved you are by Your Divine Creator, and you will cherish the closeness We can have by your remembrance of all the Blessings I bestow upon you.

My Cherished One, listen to these Words of Grace flow out from My Heart to Bless you as you endeavor to read this formidable* Book, which is truly the Manual for the Divining of Humanity.

Gratitude opens you to receive untold blessings of every kind imaginable that rain down upon you, precipitated by your thankful Worship. Contemplate My Love for you and your precious world often. Bring Me your Praise, and I will send My Grace as a Lasting Covenant, which shall lift you up to the Divine Stature of Godhood in the ages to come.

The Kingdom of Heaven shall reign in your Heart, and on the Earth, for through My Grace I have come to bring you and all humanity up to the level of Divinity. You may embark upon this Noble Career by atoning* for your sins against Mother Nature.

The Earth cries out against your wanton disregard for Her natural cycles* and the flagrant pollution of every kind that afflicts Her.

So do begin, My Beloved One, to Grace this Blessed Garden, which will bring you much Peace of Mind as you kindly Heal the Earth.

Pursue a course that is righteous and filled with gratitude, and your Heart will open with Joy to receive My Grace. There will come a time when you will be thrilled and exulted in Ecstasies of Supreme Delight, enraptured by the Blessing your Heart feels in the Infinite Reaches of Love.

My Sacred Land

Dear Ones,

Understand the fallacy of owning the land. For those of you who endeavor to control and manipulate the land for selfish gain shall surely perish. The land is not owned by any individual or corporation, nor is it owned by any nation, state, or government now on Earth. The land endures far longer than any civilization, and every earthly kingdom shall eventually fall.

The land is surely your Mother, My Blessed Ones. The most Beneficial and Sacred Endeavor you may complete is to restore the bounty of Paradise to the lands that stretch out as far as the eye can see. Yes, do repair My Blessed Treasure that I have allowed you to live upon. Truly the Earth is My Heavenly World, and all of the land does belong to God.

I AM the Creator of every infinitesimal organism that finds shelter and nourishment within My Kingdom on earth. The very life of the soil is permeated with My Divine Energy. Therefore, know this to be true: I AM the Life of the Land. I AM the Soul and the seed of the Sycamore. I AM the giant towering trees and the multitudes of grains of sand that stretch across the beaches of the world.

This land is not yours. You only pretend to own it. And the laws that you create, those that determine who may have control and ownership of the land, must change, for the earth will be shared by all of My Divine Children in the ages to come henceforth. Yes, I, your God, shall surely bless all those who honor My Sacred Land. Woe befalls those who defile their Blessed Mother.

Heaven on Earth

Dear One,

I would like to comment this day upon My Heavenly Kingdom and how it might be established upon the Earth. Yes, surely Heaven is a fine model for all of those who seek to have justice, fairness, and a sense of well-being in their lives.

Heaven's government has been tried and proven upon many worlds successfully. Therefore, I would like to give humanity, My Dear Children, the opportunity to understand this form of theocratical* government. It is more than a monarchy;* this is certain. There is room for improvement when any man or woman rules the masses. For they are placed above and beyond the common people who will eventually suffer as the imperial* monarchy taxes them.

I would rather have you embrace a monotheistic* altruistic* form of government. The same that has been established in Heaven as the perfect form of self-government for all citizens to follow. Here they express the autarchic* prerequisite displayed in your modern form of democratic* rule. My Children, each and every one of you are self-governing as far as I AM concerned, yet I do try to guide you all along the way.

It is necessary at this critical time in Earth's history to come aboard and accept the guidance that I give you at this time. Never before have so many powers maintained control over so many people's lives and determined the imperialistic* forms of government that you now embrace. There is great danger in the philosophy that "might makes right," and those with the largest arsenals of weapons have the clout to make their views and policies known and adhered to throughout the rest of the world. That is currently the situation upon your Earth where fear of destruction and self-preservation have become the ruling philosophy of the masses. This will not do. I would rather have you open your arms and your hearts and try now to understand the philosophy of the monistic* theocracy* which I give you at this time.

In Heaven, which is the name of My Kingdom, I AM Supreme. And I AM so because My concern is for the welfare of each inhabitant of My realm. Each life is precious to me. There are many who obey their inner guidance to do good, to live in peace, and to treat kindly all those they meet. This surely is the philosophy of citizenship in My Divine Realm. And this is the cornerstone of the new Heaven on Earth which I will establish now.

There must be a balance of equity within My Divine Realm: full-fledged citizenship for each and every person, plant, and animal that exists on this paradise estate. All beings shall forthwith be given permanent citizenship and shall be treated as divine heirs of this beautiful world. All men and women shall be stewards of the land. There shall be no boundaries between countries, states, or provinces.

All of the land forthwith does fall under the jurisdiction of the monotheistic theocracy of God. Heaven on Earth shall be established at this time, for My Kingdom has come on Earth, even as it is in Heaven. There are many rules of society which will benefit each and every citizen. And I plan to go over them all with you today.

Those who now hold the reigns of power shall be asked to suspend, for a time, all judgments cast upon their citizens. For I AM going to establish a new set of rules and regulations to govern all peoples and determine the welfare of each and every citizen so that people in all lands may live with the abundance and prosperity that this new government shall establish. For the welfare of each citizen is My primary concern, and unlike a king or monarch who sets himself above the common people, I AM within each one of My dearly beloved children. Therefore, I do know the hardships you face, especially with dire poverty and inequity.

There are now harsh realities that the former governments of the world have allowed to develop, and I tell you that there shall be an end to this injustice. For I do will that all of My Children, in every country and every land, embrace the ideals of Heavenly rule. The basic tenants of Heaven are for all citizens to live in peace and be kind, to demonstrate divinity and universal brother and sisterhood.

There must be a new goal for the human race. And I would establish the comfort and welfare of each and every citizen in My realm so that you may have the opportunity to discover the treasures of happiness available to each one when wealth is apparent and both abundance and prosperity are given to every one. For when the welfare of the people of all the Earth becomes the paramount goal of all humanity, then, My Dears, you have embraced the basic tenants of My Heavenly Government.

I would have you establish a fund using all of the resources of the world to draw upon and issue forth a mandate, a proclamation that all people who desire to become citizens of Heaven on Earth shall be permitted the self-governing equity* of full citizenship, subject to the rules and regulations that shall be enacted throughout the world. There shall be new laws made that shall govern all citizens, and these laws shall be based upon the code of ethics that is compatible with My Heavenly Realm. Nonviolence will be required of all citizens. And those who demonstrate violence or injure another through recklessness shall be subject to penalties and set aside from society so that they may do no more harm. There shall be freedom for all citizens to worship any way they choose, and those who have established religious practices need not change their ways. Adhering to religious ceremonies shall not be required of citizens, however; the restoration of Paradise on Earth shall become the primary objective of all citizens and everyone will be required to contribute to society. Restoring the balance of nature is the prime goal. It would be well for each and every one to enjoy many hours of leisure time each week. Therefore, citizens shall be required to work only three days per week. All shall earn the respect and admiration of society in general, whether they work as doctors, theologians, tend farms, or plant trees. All shall be respected and given the equal opportunity to serve humanity as a whole. And everyone shall earn a salary equal to the amount needed to enjoy lives filled with abundance.

Schooling shall be provided to those who would like to attend during their free time, and jobs will be given to those who request positions they would most like to fill. For instance, if someone wants to be a farmer, he or she shall have the opportunity to have an education that shall promote all of the necessary knowledge and hands-on training required to be a competent and skillful gardener. The same shall be true of those who would like to be technical engineers or inventors or those who would like to study medicine or science or any of the branches of industry, weather, or space administration.

There are very many careers for My Dear Ones to choose from, and I AM sure that many will be able to fill positions that they desire, and so, serve in a way that will bring them great happiness. There shall be a place for each one who desires to help teach those who need to learn various skills, and so I would have great universities or centers for study within communities set up and run in every locale. Those who desire to study may do so during their leisure time four days per week. They may also use their time purely for pleasure or recreation. It is important that each and every citizen be given a minimum of three months off per year for recreational purposes. This is very important. And so, My Dear Ones will work three months, three days per week, and then they shall receive a one-month vacation. At that time they may attend schools or colleges to study, or they may use this time purely to explore the world around them or devote their time to the arts or their blossoming divinity, with plenty of time for prayer, meditation, and God-contemplation.

Recreational time will be given first priority, and all citizens shall have the opportunity and ability to choose how to regulate their time so as to participate in the most joyful recreation possible. Every fifth year I would have My Dear Ones take an extended yearlong holiday to devote their time to recreation, leisure, and creativity, doing whatever it is they would most like to do. This freedom will give each and every one of My Beloved Children the opportunity to enjoy their lives. And so it is with a purposeful and divinely kind authority that I do set forth the requirements of Citizenship in Heaven on Earth. Each and every individual shall enjoy the necessities of life, paid for by the resource council.

It shall be mandated that each and every citizen shall have their basic needs met: food, clothing, shelter, and a community learning center. All will work for the good of the entire world and the good of all humanity, and all of the resources that are generated shall be freely given to the world resource council which shall dispense funds to care for each citizen. All of the money that is now held by corporations or governments or private citizens shall become the property of this resource council to dispense the basic necessities of life to each person and individual throughout this world.

All debt shall be forgiven and the vast sums of money that now go to pay the trillions of dollars of interest each year shall fund the world resource council. Thus, there will be a fresh start for each and every citizen of Heaven. All debt worldwide shall be forgiven.

Each family shall be provided a home, and the land shall be distributed so that it may be cared for by the families who occupy the land. And there shall be granted free travel abroad, and

Heaven on Earth

people shall be able to enjoy their leisure time traveling around the world if this pleases them. Each person who works in service to the whole shall be given the opportunity to enjoy an abundant life-style. This, My Dears, will contribute greatly to the health and well-being of the world and all of its people. And so, you see, there is a great opportunity to embrace a world government that works for all of its citizens while alleviating the toil of individuals everywhere.

The greatest priority must be to replant all of the beautiful countryside with trees, fruits, flowers, vineyards, groves, and orchards. Each citizen shall be required to plant 1000 trees. There shall be an agricultural commission elected to determine the best possible ways to reforest and regenerate the lands in their care. And this shall be done throughout the world. My Dear Ones shall, indeed, restore Paradise on this planet as the #1 first priority of all people.

The Blessings of Prosperity

Dear Ones,

Surely, I AM behind the Greatest Ideals that support the emergence of the world into the Golden Age of Peace. Now, as My Citizens of Heaven on Earth, you shall bring the Sacred Blessing of Prosperity to all. For as the old systems collapse, I shall offer the new way of abundance for every person on Earth. This abundance shall bring the advancement of happiness which only a privileged few experienced before this time.

Now is the time to begin this Great Age of Life, Liberty, Peace, and Abundance for all people. I shall establish the Kingdom of Heaven on Earth as all rejoice in Freedom's name. You shall have freedom from the tyranny of poverty and the shackles of fear, those unfortunate censors of Joy, Hope, and Faith. I AM the Liberty and Freedom from fear available to all now. I AM here.

To this end, I did come from My Lofty Throne in the Central Isle of Paradise. Sing of the joys all can know and will experience soon as the dawning of this Great Golden Age begins to blossom all over this world.

Come to Me, My Precious, Beloved Children. I shall release the shackles of fear created in the dungeon of poverty and give you all the riches of heavenly abundance to share and enjoy forevermore. Do this, Beloved Ones: Take your cups and fill them with the Nectar of Peace and Good Fortune I bring you. Laugh, be merry, and rejoice, for you are free at last.

A new day begins for all of you, My Beloved Ones. I shall fill your cups with the treasure of every good aspiration your heart desires, for I AM the Grantor of All Grace. Let My Grace flow out to bless all with the abundance of treasures I wish to bestow on each one. Look Me in the face and call Me by Name, I AM, the God of All Creation. I AM here. Come forth, all ye down-trodden masses, and fill your cups with the treasures of peace and understanding. Then there will be no more war. All will be free to pursue lives graced by God.

Do this for Me: Make My Name ring through the beloved, joyous places of the heart in celebration of all I have given to My Beloved Children on Earth.

Come to Me now in your perfect
peace and lovely divinity.
Fathom My blessedness.
Enjoy your treasure,
My Love for You.

The Requirements of Heaven on Earth

Dear One,

I AM so happy that you have decided to make My Spirit a part of your cherished Soul.

I would like to make you aware of the requirements necessary to create Heaven on Earth in the lives of each individual. Yes, this knowledge will have a very profound and moving effect throughout the world. For My Spirit shall live in each one of My Dear Ones as My Will is done on Earth, as Earth becomes Heaven.

There is much that needs to be done to bring this world into a state of harmony. And I tell you that the agrarian society that makes the best use of technology will be a happy middle path for humanity to walk. For it is true that although industry has polluted and tainted so very much of the natural world, still there are ways that technology can continue to grow and flourish while, at the same time, cutting out those technologies that pollute or defile the blessed atmosphere and the ground and water.

And so I tell you that the first priority for all humans who would like to become citizens of Heaven on Earth is to see what you are doing and understand the ways you are polluting the environment with your cars and machinery that now run on diesel and other fossil fuels that are eroding the precious ecosystem.

I tell you the first major change required is to
Stop Polluting the Environment
with all of the many chemicals that are destructive to life. Rather, I would have you bring forth a new technology to share the abundant energy that nature is providing every moment. Yes, StarPower solar energy will be the greatest blessing of the New Millennium, and I tell you why. For with this divine technology, there comes a way to end hunger and stop the pollution that is so rampant in so much of the world. And so please, My Dear One, do all you can to help get this

wonderful invention implemented worldwide. For the world needs it now. Do work on it and discover ways to help generate funding for this project. This invention will be shared by the people of Earth in the near future. Yes, there is a long way to go, but I assure you, it will arrive on time.

Go ahead and begin the organization now so that you can fulfill your Divine Mission and accomplish all this world needs so desperately. I will be with you Dear One, so you will be able to do much for Me, all I know you can. Take care of yourself, for there is much to do for the Kingdom of Heaven on Earth.

I will be here with you to guide you ever onward so that you can help create a new government wherein prosperity will also be an inherent right of the people, given by God. Not just the prosperity given by men, handed down through their commerce and trade. No, real prosperity based on the abundance of the land, shared by all of the people and enjoyed by everyone. This is My Goal, My Blessed One: that you add prosperity and abundance to the list of inalienable rights set down by Thomas Jefferson when the United States was born. Yes, life, liberty, abundance and prosperity, happiness, and equality among all men and women of all colors and creeds.

Yes, and add to these the blessed state of divinity, for that is also a right that I have given you. Divine you shall become, more and more, as you focus on fulfilling the needs of everyone, and less and less on satisfying the greedy destructive nature of the ego. For there can be no permanent happiness in peoples' lives as long as they are destitute, as long as they suffer in poverty and experience hunger on a daily basis.

The people suffer because the current system of commerce does not support the inalienable rights guaranteed by the Constitution of the United States of America.

I now ask you to change your commerce and Constitution to honor the directives of creating Heaven on Earth for all and transform My lovely world into a Paradise-Garden Estate. This I would have you do, My Blessed Ones. This is the destiny I have proclaimed for you all.

Heavenly Family Planning

Dear One,

It would be well for your communities to work together to assemble homes for each family. You do not have to make them all identical. Each family should be able to plan a home that will be best suited for its needs. I would have you grant single family homes to couples who desire a family when they are of the age to marry and have been well educated in family planning and parenting.

Yes, I would have each and every person who is able-bodied work for the whole of humanity. There will be no more unemployment, and there will be equal benefits for all who labor in the vast and monumental goal of Paradise-reconstruction.

Single-parent families shall have more time to rear their children. If every person works three days per week and has four days off for recreation and leisure, or schooling if desired, there will be plenty of time for children to spend with their own parents. And even those parents who need to be with their children full-time while they are young can contribute to society by planting flowers or tending vineyards and taking their children with them.

There shall be a great beautification project as all people endeavor to create Paradise here once again. And I would have you all do everything within your power to beautify this abundant land. By so doing, you shall restore the beautiful vistas that shall inspire you everywhere you go.

I would have you give first consideration to those who need the most. Yes, My Dears, there is a great inequity here now. And I would have you, first and foremost, do for those who have more need than others.

I would have each family keep its main residence as its home. Other homes should be given to their children or neighbors and distributed more evenly. There is no need for one person or one family to own twenty homes and rent them out. No, My Dears, it would be better for each family to enjoy having one home and caring for that home and maintaining it while using their time and energy to help create a world of wonder and a beneficial environment for everyone. Yes, meeting the goal of creating Paradise here is more important than any other pursuit, and more needed. For, as this world is ushered into the Golden Age, you shall receive the Blessings of Love and know what it means to share and give your energy to developing the perfect situation for each and every one of My Divine Family.

And so, please do all you can to make the goal of prosperity for each person a tribute to Me. For I do want to have all of My Children nurtured and well fed. And I AM sure you have this capability within your power, if you will just make having Heaven on Earth a priority.

Every Desire Fulfilled

There is enough for everyone on this dear planet to be rich in spirit and have abundance, including health and all of the material necessities of life. So do, please, take this time to begin anew and restructure your society to meet the needs of the people, thereby bringing a great peace, the peace that comes from having all you need.

Every desire fulfilled shall be the buzzwords of the new millennium. Every Desire Fulfilled. Yes, My Dear, every worthwhile desire can be fulfilled as you proceed to make the best out of everything you have and make sure that everyone receives all that is needed to live in happiness, health, and abundance. Then, surely, you will find yourselves in My Divine Kingdom, and Heaven will be restored upon this blessed world. For I AM here now to reorder worldly affairs in the way of divinity. And you shall profit from knowing the requests and recieving the guidance of your God in the days to follow.

My Blessed One, hear Me when I say that all is being made ready for your entrance into the Golden Age of God, when there will be no more war or persecution of any of My Children. I would have you know that you are all My precious and beloved children, every one of you. So do kindly honor each one of your dear brothers and sisters on this world, and all the worlds to follow. For many other civilizations will be revealed to you when you are living this basic tenant of brotherhood.

As a global family, you will organize a divine trust which is designed to create Paradise on Earth. This trust will hold sacred every life, and all the land will be used to recreate the gardens of God, which were on this Earth some 38,000 years ago. So do, please, make this Paradise your priority, and I will be with you to guide you and give you inspiration and health at every turn.

I do wish you all a blessed day. May your lives be filled with peace and joy and may your hearts be gladdened because I AM with you. I will always be here for you to turn to in these next few precious years, upon which the balance of nature hangs. It is up to you to restore the forests of Paradise upon this world. I AM counting on you to do this for Me.

I AM guiding each and every one of My Children to the summit of perfection, and you shall all know what it means to be Godly in the days soon to follow. I will tell you exactly how it will be when you endeavor to bring forth the Love of God into your heart at all times. It will be a blessed gift to all the people of the world to behold My Love firsthand. As you begin to feel Me within your Soul, I would have you know that I AM here to offer you all of the Love your heart can hold and all of the joy that you may embrace.

The Sanctuary you shall construct in My Name shall be the Divine Gathering Place for all of My Blessed Ones who seek to worship the Divine Nature within themselves and each other. For I AM present within the hearts and minds of each of My Blessed Children. And I do want to be acknowledged. I want to be the goal of My Blessed Children, who can merge with Me and become My Divine Emissaries unto the world.

Yes, I have a wonderful plan in store for each and every one of you. And I do hope that you will soon be successful in manifesting a Sanctuary of Divine Love, where you may all join together and give thanks for all I give you. Have as a focal point of your service the Divine Communion of Christ. Partaking of His Holy

Grail will be a blessed event for you to look forward to each week. And I tell you that these Sanctuaries you shall gather in to celebrate your love of God will be focal points for the community efforts needed to restore Paradise here. And so, I do encourage you to gather My Lambs together and bring them in from the cold of modernistic society so they may warm themselves in the light of My Love.

Let there be no more greed, wanton sin, or degradation, for those filled with greed are surely unconscious of the premier aspects of Love. And intolerance, spread through use of false doctrines and beliefs, shall perish forevermore to be replaced by My Divine Love and My Perfect Words for all the world to hear.

I do want My Words brought forth for humanity's benefit, for there is nothing which is more important than the advancement of the consciousness of humanity. For therein lies the key to the safety and preservation of the Earth and all of its bountiful resources, which may be shared to bring peace and contentment to everyone. This new government, My Dear, is the establishment of My Divine Kingdom, The Kingdom of Heaven on Earth.

Yes, it is true that Heaven shall be manifest upon the Earth within the next decade. And this shall come about because of your earnest efforts. And your joyous Sanctuary shall be a place of happiness where My Divine Family can gather together and celebrate Our Love and Kinship. For I AM here with you all. Everyone of you has My Divine Spirit at the core of your being. And I would have you realize My Divine Presence and receive the title of My Name:

I AM.

I AM

I AM here within you

Deep within you there is a God. I AM the God of Paradise. I AM the Bringer of Hope. I AM the Creator of All That Is. I AM the Enlightener of Humanity and the Prince of Peace. I AM here, and I AM pleased with this accomplishment.

Feel My presence reaching forth from you like the rays of the sun, shining, radiating glorious light through you into the world of corruption and darkness. Become My divine pillar of light who summons the glory of God made manifest in human form. Undaunted, let your Spirit sing. Enjoy its refrains, for I AM here. I AM in you, My Darling. And these great truths will soon be known and experienced by My Dear Hearts all around the world.

Honor your Father in Heaven by bringing My divine light into the world as you go about your day, this day, and always henceforth. Align yourself with My divinity and breathe Me in consciously as you bring forth godliness as a beacon that shines within, illumining the divine and sacred sanctuary of the heart with peace and joy and love. Let Me fill you, My Dear. Let Me honor you and your perfect trust.

Enjoy all I have given you and create the bountiful treasure of Heaven on Earth for everyone through your efforts. Yes, persevere, My Darling Heart, and make this presence of God's own Spirit known unto the world through you this day.

Guardian of Paradise

Do all you can, My Dear. Become the Guardian of Paradise who will always benefit the Earth and all that lives. Change your mind to reflect the perfect and divine attributes of love toward every being, place, person, and object, and all things shall flow together in a blessing of harmonious interaction that will inspire and delight and bring spontaneity to all of My Children everywhere.

I AM so grateful that you have chosen to listen to the message of your Lord this day. It is wise of you to begin to live your life anew and bring forth the treasure and bounty of heaven into every home. Set your sights on accomplishing all you may for the great glory of God and bring forth an era of peace and ultimate perfection to this world of Mine.

Restoring Paradise on Earth

Dear Ones,

Truly, I do have a plan to restore Paradise on Earth. This plan is held in trust by My Emissary, I AM. I have given her the blueprint for the reconstruction of this global Paradise within your lifetimes. It is up to you to do all you can to assist in the reforestation of this world with beautiful ornamental plants, as well as varied fruits, nuts, seeds, and flowering botanicals. These will provide a park-like beauty of natural loveliness to lands now occupied by cattle and mono-crops, which denude the soil and erode its life-giving properties.

To be specific, I AM counting on you to change your world and restore the Paradise that has been lost through expropriation* by profiteers whose only motives are greed, and who lack the basic fundamental morality to coexist with nature. It is wise for you to plan to spend your days beautifying this war-torn world. The war on nature must end. Now is the time to rebuild your Paradise Home.

It is wise that you discontinue using rivers as dumping grounds for all waste and human feces. The rivers were meant to be a clean source of water for you to drink and irrigate your fields, to swim and bathe in, and for you to enjoy the purity they bring. Do not pollute them anymore!

There are ways to restore the vitality of the earth. Use powder-fine rock dust to fertilize the soil, and the sun-dried natural wastes of animals and humans spread upon the ground and turned into the soil. Spirulina and other blue green algae grown in the StarPower energy stations will also be used as fertilizers to increase the productivity of the land so all may enjoy the rich bounty and extraordinary beauty of this Paradise World of Heaven.

I have provided the solution to your worlds' energy problems. I would have you energize your homes and automobiles with electrical power generated by the StarPower invention I have entrusted to My Emissary, which will provide the basic necessities of energy, pure water, and food for everyone to share and enjoy. This invention will end world hunger and bring prosperity to all the inhabitants of Earth. Do construct many StarPower stations around the globe, and you will all benefit greatly from this noble endeavor.

StarPower is a clean energy invention which manufactures abundant electricity through use of Solar and OTEC - ocean thermal energy conversion. I have inspired My Emissary, I AM, with this clean energy invention for a Global Solar Utility to provide people everywhere with safe, clean electrical power, fresh pure water, and rich vegetable protein - the basic necessities of life for all. Among the resources StarPower will provide are sea minerals, aqua-culture, fish nurseries, marine farming, and fresh water for irrigation and revitalization of deserts, Utilizing StarPower, and remineralizing and reforesting the planet will result in the resurrection of Paradise and lay the foundation for the Kingdom of Heaven on Earth.

The Divine Self
slays the greedy destructive nature
of the beast called ego to attain
Heaven on Earth

Divine Justice

Dear One,

Verrily, I AM here. I AM the Divine Light bringing salvation to the many Blessed Ones who seek My Presence. I AM the Giver of Life and the Keeper of the Sacred Flame of Divine Love. I AM the Guardian of the Meek and the Upholder of Truth and Justice. I AM the Deliverer of the multitudes from ignorance to Enlightenment. I AM the Perfect God of All Creation. I AM the Savior of the ecosystems of Earth. I AM establishing the Inaugural Commencement of Adjudication* in the Sovereign* Reign of My Kingdom on Earth.

I will bring justice and order to the world of men who carry out the Laws of the Land, the Law of Ethics in particular, for ethics will be demanded of all those who hold offices or positions of power.

Come unto Me all My Children who have waged war against nature and be cleansed of your sins. Stop crippling nature for monetary gain. You are creating vile plagues by rampant pollution, herbicides, insecticides, radioactive wastes, and errant agri-business practices involving the use of antibiotics, hormones, and the cruel unsanitary crowding of animals. Many more diseases stem from viral strains created in laboratories for use in biological warfare.

These actions can no longer be tolerated by this Administration of Mine. A process shall commence to end the suffering of the natural world at the hands of corrupt individuals who commit unscrupulous acts of wanton destruction, atmospheric degradation, and biological warfare.

I AM here and I do demand that all such acts of criminal intent against nature be halted. These atrocities require immediate rectifying. A remedy for the elimination of these poisonous wastes must be discovered and utilized to bring all systems into balance and a state of health so that the natural world will be vindicated.* Forthcoming Justice will be sought by individuals who protect the environment. Righteous Laws will be made to protect and indemnify* nature.

Do not think that the Righteous Judgment of those who profit by the genocide of My Creatures and the life of the land itself is harsh, for it is My Tenderest Mercy shown forth to stave off* the insolent acts of wanton destruction perpetrated against the land. My Children, I would have you realize that My Infinite Mercy does dispense Divine Justice, for without it, all would be lost and the Life of the Land would be no more.

This Perfect Paradise Home I created for you must not be allowed to be destroyed. Therefore, I would have you make new laws to set aside great tracts of land to be shared for the benefit of all people. In this way you may sponsor the creation of Paradise once again.

Do this for Me, My Chosen Ones, bring forth your Divinity and hold the Land Sacred and Honor this precious living and breathing world.

I would have you know that there is no one alive who can will the land to bring forth life in great abundance. That is a Divine Perogative. The enduring life shall flow out from My Divine Kingdom blessing all. In My Holy Endeavor to provide the cherished answer to Earth's ills, this I shall do, My Blessed Ones.

Protect the Meek

That man tries to justify in his attempt to disparage* those in need will not stand up as lawful in the judgement of the High Tribunal of Love, Mercy, and Righteousness.

Many good people in history have been led by their inner Spirit to do what I inspired them to do, and often their actions have gone against the current establishment. Going against the grain is the way people effect change. Man's laws are often made to serve only those who can afford to get them passed. It is only when enough of these inequitable laws injure a majority of the people that things finally change. Men and women sometimes have to stand up for what is right, even though their struggle is in defiance of established, yet unfair practices.

Men will never know the full meaning behind the events that are blessed by the Creator. This painting of the Women of Sabine depicts a time when I sequestered* an entire battalion, a regiment of soldiers on the battle field by inspiring the women to step in.

They were warring over unfair practices by feudal land lords who taxed them unjustly, yet afforded them no citizenship, shelter, or help when they were disabled. It was just such a battle that inspired many men to give up their lives rather than be dictated to in this insolent* manner. It was a fearsome battle. The banners were flying for those who could no longer care for themselves. It was a valiant struggle in which the awesome forces were displayed in such a way that right did ensue.

Now there are many disabled homeless people suffering on the streets because of the unfair practices of those who make unjust rulings to suit their pocketbooks.

New laws must be passed to protect nature and the human rights of all. Do all you can in this effort to protect the meek, whether they be people, animals, or the citizens of the seas who are threatened with extinction due to mankind's erring ways. The environment must be protected for the benefit of all of earth's living treasures, so you may all live and share the abundance I have blessed you with.

My Chosen Ones, pass ethical laws to govern your world with Love and Divine Mercy towards all.

My ethical lawmakers, do not give up, for I know where your hearts lie. This battleground on which you must stand is for the fairness, the ethics, and honor that can only be won in the judicial arena. The battlefield is being readied for a supernal conquest which shall liberate the ones who have been defiled for so long; those who are meek and have given up hope of salvation; those who suffer in needless poverty; those innocents who are hunted relentlessly to extinction; those who have been slain by agri-businesses destroying the Amazon to raise cattle which further deforest and denude the land. This destruction of your planet's rainforests is environmental suicide. It must be stopped! The balance of nature hangs on your actions in the next few years. Trees supply the oxygen you breathe and burn to power your automobiles and machines and to generate your electricity. There is an oxygen deficit of millions of metric tons each year.

It is time to stop producing emissions that poison the air and rob oxygen from the ozone shield. Massive reforestation projects must be instituted globally to reinstate the oxygen and stop the greenhouse effect. All humanity must cooperate in this effort by passing universal laws that will ensure the continuation of life on earth. Go about your day, legislators, and do all in accordance with My Divine Will.

The Law of Karma

Dear Ones,

egarding Karma: "For every action, there is an equal and opposite reaction." What you do literally comes back to you. "What goes around, comes around." "As you sow, so shall you reap what you sow." These proverbs* describe the Law of Karma. That is why the Golden Rule Jesus taught is so very important: "Do unto others as you would have them do unto you." For the way you treat others is the way you shall be treated later on. Being conscious of one's actions minimizes ill-effects of past negative actions, however, you really must "pay the piper."

This law is irrevocable throughout all creation and must be dealt with to align the flow of good actions begetting good reactions for a secure future. If you have been experiencing a slew of problems in your life, take the time to understand just why and how these situations may be related to the actions that preceded them. This query will lead to understanding and subsequent release from the negative effects of karma. Once you see how to create "good karmic reactions" by consciously creating them, you may live in relative peace and prosperity.

It is true that "what goes around comes around," so be sure to always act kindly in every situation and, especially, do not judge those living in the backlash of their karmic problems, for all are susceptible to judgment. Judge not, least ye be judged, for judgment reveals a superior attitude which can only result in disaster.

"The higher you are, the further you fall" is true when relating to the false bolstering of the ego created by judging and putting others below you. This cannot be done without serious repercussions. It eventually leads to the suffering of the individual who first felt superior. This injurious attitude is the most prevalent of all "holier than thou" egotistic aggrandizement* problems, for this Attitude will cause a backlash as surely as it was perpetrated.* "Gossip, even the name hisses," for truly, the lashing out of self-righteous, judgmental tongues reaps the backlash of the whip that stings the most. So never wantonly discredit another or viciously use words as curses, for curses return to their masters, like evil winds that bring the house down and leave them accused and naked in shame.

"Forgive and you shall be forgiven." This prescription is the way to relieve the effects of post-karmic blues. You may take the time to do it right and relieve a lifetime of karmic debt in a few weeks. If you are diligent and persevering, you may accomplish this task in three weeks of concentrated effort. By relieving this load of karmic debt, a whole new and better future will open up to receive you as a karma-free Soul.

> Forgive...
> and you shall be forgiven.

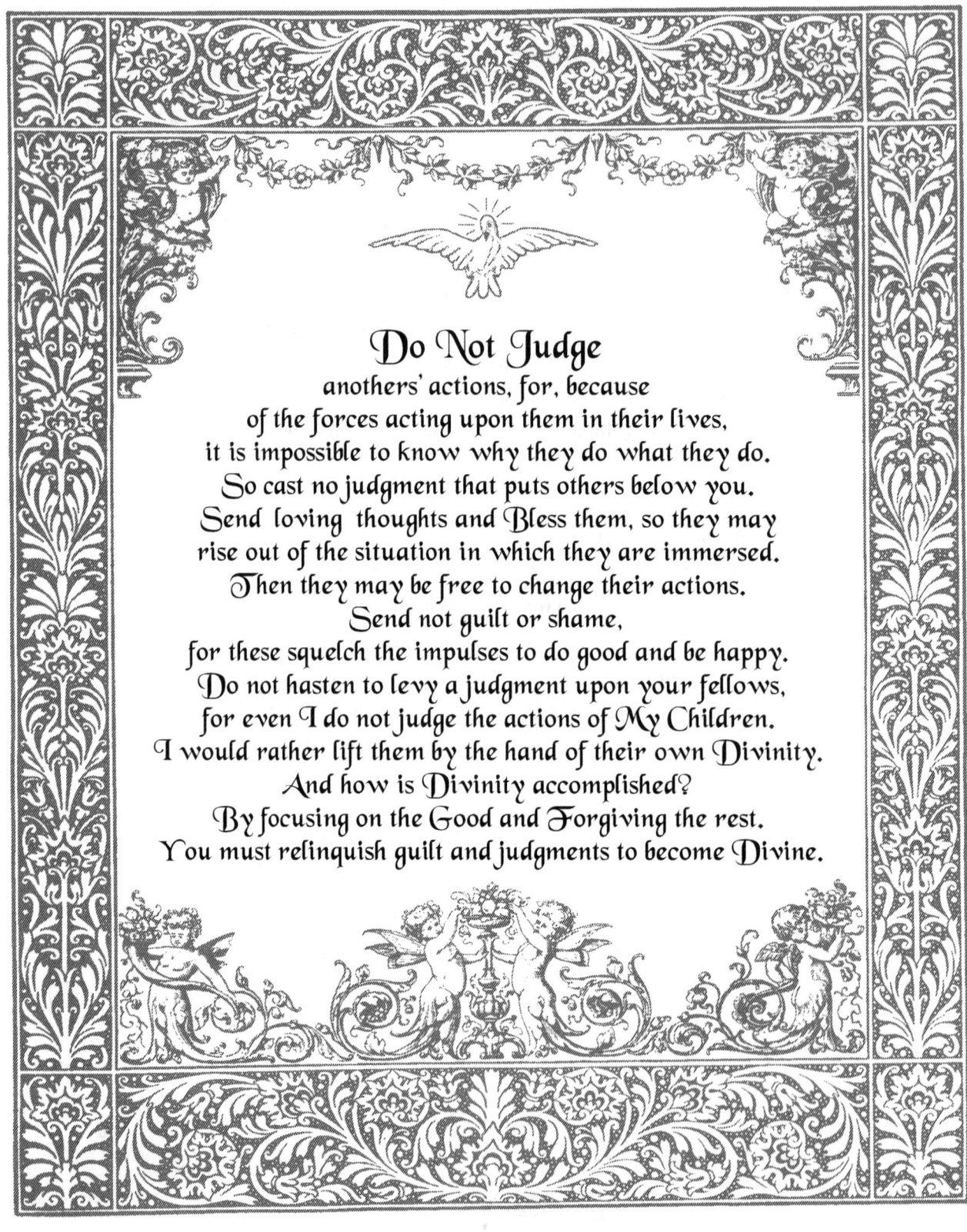

Do Not Judge

anothers' actions, for, because
of the forces acting upon them in their lives,
it is impossible to know why they do what they do.
So cast no judgment that puts others below you.
Send loving thoughts and Bless them, so they may
rise out of the situation in which they are immersed.
Then they may be free to change their actions.
Send not guilt or shame,
for these squelch the impulses to do good and be happy.
Do not hasten to levy a judgment upon your fellows,
for even I do not judge the actions of My Children.
I would rather lift them by the hand of their own Divinity.
And how is Divinity accomplished?
By focusing on the Good and Forgiving the rest.
You must relinquish guilt and judgments to become Divine.

Judgments

Beloved One,

I AM with you in all you say and do. Make My Presence known through all your Universe as the Divine One who sees all, and knows the reason behind every action; the Silent Witness who sees every deed, knows every motive, and hears every thought. I AM the Divine Personality of the Godhead who listens to the pleas of My Dear Children everywhere and brings solace to the Pilgrims who make their journey inward, drawn to My Perfection.

Come to Me, My Darling One, and do not hasten to levy* a judgment upon your fellows, for I AM also resident within the hearts and minds of each one of My Dearly Beloved Children.

Look beyond the outer frame and past the ignorance of those who know Me not. So judge not, nor levy a judgment of dross* or ill-intent, for I AM here, My Darling One. I AM the Basis of each one of you. I AM the Divine Person you are becoming.

Know this: I will always judge you with the Divine Perspective of a Holy Parent, one who always sees the beauty you have within you, the Spark of Divinity to burn through the dross and become a citizen of Paradise, who shall inherit My Glorious Kingdom and all the Treasures I AM.

So lift up your gaze beyond the outer mundane appearance of your fellows and behold the Christ within each one who is becoming more like Me with each passing breath, for I AM the Divine Destination of each and every one of My Beloved Beings.

Turn to Me. Come home, My Chosen One. I love you so much. Paradise rings with the Bells of Freedom. Freedom from lack and pain, freedom from the dross, freedom to sing, to laugh, and to enjoy your life forevermore.

Kindness

Dear One,

Hearken* unto Me, for I will give you the basic recipe of the Divine Spirit. Just as your physical body requires sustenance, so does your Soul. Nurture your Spirit with the ingredients of Love: Kindness and Compassion sweetened by Charity, Hope, and Faith, and divined with Altruism,* Philanthropy,* and Perseverance. And all of this crowned with Trust, Truth, and Goodness.

An intangible yet ample nourishment comes from partaking of the Heavenly Graces, which are the Divine Foods your Soul requires to grow healthfully. Each time you choose to offer Kindness to one of your fellows in need of such a Grace, your reward is a strengthening morsel of Soul Food, which you require to survive mortal death and create the Immaculate

Spirit you are becoming. These Heavenly Foods divine your Soul, and your natures are blessed by expressing these delightful qualities throughout your lives.

Thus begins the building of your Immortal Soul's Body of Light, and it will Glorify you more and more by your frequent choices to do good and be happy. As you demonstrate these God-like Attributes of Spirit and incorporate them into your mind and heart, you feed your Soul. Just as surely as earthly food builds strong bodies, these ingredients will provide you with all you need to express the finer, higher ideals which are reachable.

When you can stand on the sure-footing of these Noble Attributes, you will begin to feel the more Idealistic Currents of Spirit lifting you to the Realms of the Angels, and on to the Home of the Godly. Yes, these Divine Attributes are surely the steps of Jacob's Ladder, for when you express them, they build your character and become part of your life. By expressing them often, you may step up to a new level of consciousness, moving onward and upward to the Summit of Divinity expressed and experienced only by the gods and goddesses of Paradise.

I would have you practice these Divine Attributes often, for they do nourish your Soul and cause you to grow in Spirit and become more and more like your Heavenly Father each day.

Mercy

Dear One,

ercy is the greatest beneficent Grace, and it is My Pleasure to bring it into your life and heart. It is true that there is a great deal you have gained from the Bestowal of Mercy upon your Soul. The adjudication* of the Souls of humanity is tempered by My unending Mercy throughout the worlds made by the Hands of My Divine Son, Jesus. Mercy is His trademark. Love is His duty. Your whole universe, Nebadon, which is located in the seventh super universe of Orvonton, is indeed, pervaded by the stabilizing forces of Mercy and Love. These are the predominating energy fields dominating the Divine Life Currents in your sector of the Grand Universe.

Mercy and Love are the gifts of the kindest heart and it is wise for you to become the official bestower of this wonderful remedy. Mercy comes through Compassion, and Forgiveness is its keynote. Do foster relationships filled with Love and Mercy, for this combination is the Great Redeemer* of Souls. I would have you practice this Noble Attribute, Mercy as a character refining tool. Bring home this marvelous healing balm and utilize it in your daily life so you can master the most wonderful aspects of consciousness to make your Soul Divine.

Be kind, in all you say and do, and relish* the Divine Attribute of Forgiveness, for this is surely Mercy in action. I would have you find this Great Redeemer and bestow it upon those who have injured you, for Forgiveness is the blessing that brings the Divine Gift of Mercy into the lives of individuals, releasing them from guilt and karmic repercussions. Dear One, I AM here for you at every turn and I will be most happy to assist you in relinquishing the dross and acquiring the Attribute of Mercy that is so essential to your Soul's development.

I AM the Way, the Truth and the Light. Surely you will know Me by My Unending Mercy in the days to come, when this world is transformed, once again, into Paradise. It shall be accomplished by My Beloved Ones, who now choose to embrace the Divine Attributes, which you are becoming so accustomed to, as I grace your Soul with the unending capacity to bestow Kindness at every turn upon your fellows and those who have hurt you in any way.

Relinquish the dross, oh My Blessed One. Find Me here within your heart, for I AM the bringer of the good, glad tidings, and I will elevate you as you embrace these Divine Attributes and find them within your Soul. Soon you will realize that Compassion, Forgiveness, Mercy, and Love are the very cornerstones of your being, for they are truly who you are. My Beloved, you have embodied My Holy Spirit and your Soul is becoming more Divine as you embrace these Ideals that formulate the basis of your divining character.

I AM the Truth that shall set you free. I AM the Joy that shall fill your heart with Divine Gladness. I AM the Divine Mercy that shall forgive every sin and erring way. I AM the Divine Liberation you shall experience as you spread your Wings of Spirit and soar into My Lofty Heavens, to come to My Side in Paradise. I AM the Divine Keeper of your Soul and the One who bestows Eternal Life for right-choosing. Therefore, come unto Me, My Chosen One, and express the Tender Mercy you are endowed with.

In the days ahead you will experience the Divine Mercy of My Holy Grace. Receive this unconditionally, for it is true there is no past you must regret, or future you must fear. For I AM here with you now and My Plan is to bring you the Heavenly Graces, so you may incorporate them in your life and express the Divinity I AM, in you and through you, to this precious world of Mine and all the Blessed Residents thereof. You shall prosper in the days ahead by acquiring this Divine and Noble Attribute of Being, for Mercy will surely follow you all the days of your life.

Sanctify Life

Do Not Kill,
Neither human beings, nor birds,
nor members of the animal kingdom.
They are all precious to Me.
I would rather have you
treat them with respect
and honor their lives
as you honor the life
I have given you.

Live in Peace

My Divine Law

Dear One,

How may you honor Me when man's laws are opposed to God's laws? This is a formidable ethical question. It is often the curse of humanity to follow laws that are created by those who seek control and dominion over their fellows.

My Divine Law is that you should live, prosper, and grow in Spirit as you become more like Your Father in Heaven each and every day. These Divine Prerequisites to your human success are well met in the Bounty that comes forth as you endeavor to do My Will. Doing so leads the way for great understanding and brings peace and solace into troubled hearts.

As in all times that have gone before, there have been many who required the killing of others to perpetrate acts of war and conquest. Even though there have been laws requiring mandatory drafting of citizens for warfare, I would have you all realize that this is truly against My Law, for killing another is not what I would have you do at any time.

My Beloved One, there have been many times in history when sacrifice was deemed a sacred law to honor My Almighty Power. Many beautiful and innocent Darlings have been crucified or slain in gruesome ways by men who sought to appease Me. These sacrifices are blasphemies in My Sight and I AM forever grateful that this practice has ended among most of the peoples of Earth, who have finally evolved beyond this gruesome enterprise.

I first spoke to Moses to ask him to relate My Divine Laws to the people of his day. My First Law was that of nonviolence. "Thou shalt not kill" was My Preeminent Decree. It was inevitable that these laws should be broken, for they were given at a time when men were at a primitive level of cultural morality. Only a few thousand years have passed and yet, look how you have grown. I asked Moses to have humans stop killing each other as well as their animal fellows.

However, he could not deliver My Laws to his people at that time, for he sincerely believed that these ignorant former slaves could not have possibly followed My Divine Laws, so he tempered them with his own translation. He was partly successful, for with the laws he brought forth, the acts of human sacrifice were ended. However, people still sought to appease My Almighty Power by sacrificing their tiny lambs and the best of their flocks and the choicest of their oxen. These killings are an abomination* in My Sight, and I have sincerely regretted that this practice has continued on for so many years during which people killed other creatures mistakenly believing they were appeasing Me.

My other Laws are related in this Divine Book of Revelation. Herein are My 20 Requests for you to follow in your daily lives. By doing so, you will surely manifest perfection, and the blessed state of Heaven shall reign within your heart and will grace this planet.

Heaven on Earth

Paradise on Earth

Take the time to begin, in all you say and do, to relinquish the dross* and ennoble* your heart by endeavoring to follow My 20 Requests. Obeying My Commandments will bring you the Divine Gifts you so desire and create Heaven in your midst. This is My Will for you.

It is true that I have given every possible inspiration so you may realize this Divine Ideal of Peace in your life. Do give thanks and praise for the Peacemakers who have enabled this first transformation to occur on Earth as the Golden Age of God begins.

Come home to Heaven, My Darling One, and reside in the place where peace unfolds naturally amongst peoples and nations who are centered on these Divine Ideals which I AM bestowing upon you in this Divine Age you are embarking upon now.

Hold these Covenants sacred, My Beloved One, and you shall live in splendor, for Paradise shall reign on Earth, even as it does in Heaven.

Cherish these Words I have given you, for they are the Perfect Revelation of My Divine Mind, and I bring you the feeling of My Perfect Love through My Thoughts.

Relinquish the dross, O My Beloved One, and you will soon soar on Wings of Love and know happiness beyond all measure.

Your Daily Bread

Dear One,

For a time, eat no meat, and you will gain the trust of the animals that sense if a carnivore is near. The birds will adore you for this cleansing of your aura. Fish is meat too, and so is fowl. Eat from the garden where plants grow willingly for your sustenance. Remember, if it runs away from you, you are not meant to eat it. The fruits and vegetables, grains, beans, and nuts do grow for your table. Eat these and abjure* the use of meat, for it is a poison to your Spirit to take the life of a creature that desires to live. There is Plenty to eat and drink. The Banquet of Nature shall be your Feast.

I AM the Provider of all that grows. I AM the Health of the Ecosystem. I AM the Vitality you feel and express. So do this for Me: Keep your Diet simple. Eat the herbs of the fields, the fruits of the trees, the abundance of the garden, and the rich diversity of the plant kingdom. This I have given you for your food, not the animals. They are here to keep you company, to be your friends and allies, so you do not get lonely; to protect you and help you carry your burdens. This I also ask: Feed not your pets the fish of the sea, for they are almost gone. Make your kibbles from plankton and other rich vegetable sources. The kittens will thrive and puppies will be strong and healthy; there is no need to kill off the last of the fish for your pets.

These fish need to live and become healthy again. They are contaminated with poisonous metals and infected with chemical pollutants. My Divine Up-stepping of the waters with Divine Life Currents shall give them the strength to survive and flourish again. Please stop fishing. Dine for a time at My Gardens. The trees love to nurture you. Make this fruit your food.

When Adam and Eve materialized I spoke to Adam and gave him the herbs of the fields and fruits of the trees to be the diet (meat) for mankind. Surely, this information has been lost to the people of Earth. My Children do not even know how to feed themselves. They are certainly not yet Godly enough to restructure the balance of nature while they appease their appetites with game and cattle, which is detrimental to the balance of nature.

This do for Me, My Darling Heart: Do not injure or kill other creatures. They love their lives, just as you do. They are sacred, too. It was never meant for you to kill them in such a wholesale slaughter of Life.

Do not kill is My First Commandment. This I did give to Moses when he came to find Me at Mount Sinai. There were Ten Commandments then that Moses requested his people to follow and keep. The flesh pots were burning then, filled with the meat of their sacred cattle, which they made into their god. Their golden idol was destroyed at that time and the cruelty of killing animals was supposed to stop. This was not accomplished, however, and now the wholesale slaughter of animals everywhere has reached epic proportions. This is not My Will, My Children. Thou shalt not kill means

Thou Shalt Not Kill!

Life begets life; death begets death. When you eat a dead animal, fish or bird, your sense of divinity can never fully be expressed through you. Killing is a sin and the wages of sin are death. The bacteria that proliferates upon the carrion of dead animals is poisonous to the human digestive tract. Over time, it shortens the life span. People used to live a thousand years. Methuselah ate only fruits and vegetables, herbs and water. As people began eating cooked meat, their life spans shortened dramatically. It takes too much vital energy to deal with the toxins animal carrion produces in the human body, thus shortening the life span of My Children and making them unhealthy and unclean.

An unclean body cannot house an Immaculate Spirit. Dross prevents direct communication with My Indwelling Holy Spirit and cripples the progress of Spiritual Attainment needed to transcend mortal death and survive as a Spirit Being.

Please stop the wholesale slaughter of animals that is causing the destruction of nature. I have a better way in mind. Follow Me and we shall recreate Heaven on Earth. My Blessed Child, do this for Me.

Replant the Trees

Do not take the lives of the trees.
They are needed to
restore the balance of nature.
I would have every person now alive
plant an assortment of fruit and nut trees.
They will provide your banquet in Paradise.
Propagate them and you will be blessed.

Do this for Me, O My Chosen Ones:
Begin this day the work of
Paradise reconstruction.

Save The Trees

oved One,

My Supreme Request is that you reforest this world that humanity has denuded of the life-giving trees needed to produce the atmosphere you breathe. It is My Will for you to abandon the annihilating practices now employed to clear vast tracts of land each day, for these will surely lead to environmental suicide.

Please restore My Forests and bring Peace back to the biosphere, for the trees determine how the winds blow, and the rains fall and prevent the Age of Ice from enveloping the land.

It is time to begin anew to formulate the Divine Directives I AM giving you. I request that each and every person now alive take the time to plant an assortment of fruit and nut bearing trees. This replanting will be the restitution required for your species to continue to live on Earth and dwell in My Paradise once more.

Begin anew to create the perfect Paradise envisioned by those of you who are inspired by My Divine Spirit. Begin to understand the quality of life that may be experienced as a result of this great endeavor. You shall all prosper from this Divine Work in the times soon to come when you embark upon the Sacred Destiny of establishing Heaven on Earth. Restore My Gardens and you shall be blessed.

Do not toil for the suffering of any living thing, whether it be a person, plant or animal. Regard the Earth as your mother and do not poison her with chemicals, nor deface her with bombs and other implements of destruction. Do not deforest, for the killing of a tree is a sin, and those who kill trees will themselves be cut down and survive not the roll call of justice.

Come to Me, all My Children who have waged war against nature and be cleansed of your sins. Stop the endless torture of the tree kingdom. Do this for Me: I beseech you to help end this slaughter. Bring an end to the immense suffering of nature. There has never been a time when there has been the extinction of so many species due to habitat deforestation. The suffering must end. I Will it to be so. My Emissary, I AM, will be forthcoming with an answer to this senseless slaughter and bring an end to the immense suffering of nature.

Hear Me now, O Divine Ones. I AM here to begin this world anew and you are My Chosen Legions of Earth Guardians who will protect and defend the biosphere in My Name. Go forth and bring Me the fruits of your labors that will grow, flower, and bloom as you restore Earth to a Garden Paradise so lovely that you will all be graced with profound beauty at every turn.

Do this for Me, O My Chosen Ones: Begin this day to endeavor the work of Paradise reconstruction. Do it for your Lord who does desire your happiness and contentment. Paradise is possible! And you will see the fruits of your labors bring forth the Glorious Gardens of God to grace this world of Heaven.

Begin to hold the lives of trees as sacred,
and you shall become Guardians of the Destiny of your world.

Guardians of Destiny

Dear Ones,

There are available to you many fine alternatives to trees for homes, paper products, furniture, household items, and instruments made of wood. You may substitute a quality resin made from the distilling of recycled materials that have already been used in some other form. Many plastics are available for this use and can be designed to look exactly like wood.

Ferrocement* can be used to construct storm-proof homes and temples in a variety of architectural designs. Even boats can be made of this creative material, which allows freedom of design.

There are many plants that can be made into paper. Papyrus grows well in the shallows of rivers. Hemp grows well across the land and could be utilized for all your paper needs. Cotton can also be used to form paper products, especially when combined with the former. Clothing may be created from these natural fibers as well.

So do be creative, My Beloveds. You have every natural talent for creating what you need. Many products are available that you may utilize, including the reuse of many materials now being wasted in landfills and being dumped into the ocean where they cause pollution.

Trees are often used as a source of fuel for fires, to cook food, and heat homes. There are many alternatives to this wholesale destruction of the trees, which take so very long to mature. There are ovens made of brick and glass, which will allow baking with solar radiation. I would suggest that these and other alternatives be employed.

Fire for heat will no longer be required when the StarPower* Solar Energy technology is in place. Clean safe electric power will be supplied by this natural conveyance,* bringing satisfaction to every hearth, as homes are well lit and warmed through the use of abundant free energy which will become available to all Earth's citizens in the near future. To save the biosphere, I urge you to switch to electric automobiles and replace all polluting machinery with this Godsend.

Take special care of My Precious Trees, the Mahogany and Teak, the Cedars and Redwoods, for they are almost extinct, and these Precious Ones that have lived so long gracing the Earth will be sorely missed should their genocide be allowed to continue. Take heart, My Darling Ones, you have resources available to you now. The seeds these great trees produce may be used to reforest denuded lands.

In the future times, you will all be blessed to partake of your Divine Mother through Her Emissaries, the Trees. Through these the Earth will feed you and provide the air you breathe. So make a pact to begin to hold the lives of trees as sacred, and you shall become Guardians of the Destiny of your world.

"You must be like little children
to see the wonders of Heaven." ...Jesus

Simplicity

Dear Ones,

Simplicity is a joyful Attribute to have. It is so wonderful when any of My Children can demonstrate this blessed quality within their lives and consciousness. The less complicated one's life is, the more room there is to express Joy. Jesus said, "You must be like little children to see the wonders of Heaven,"

So keep your lives simple, My Darling Ones. Choose to let go of the complicated lives which leave you stressed and afraid. There is a simple life dawning on your horizon: Life in the Garden of God. Getting back to nature can simplify your lives greatly, My Cherished Ones.

I would have you plan to simplify your lives so you can accommodate more time for play and enjoyment of this Beloved World. I would also have you use your leisure time to come to Me often in God-Contemplation and bring Me the sweet gift of your Love, for this I do cherish above all else. It is said, "What does it profit a man to gain the whole world if he loses his Soul?" This Truth is as wise now as it was in days of old.

The Simple Treasures are bountiful and liberating. I would have you enjoy these great treasures, My Darlings, and you will notice a change in your lifestyles which will bring a fonder relationship between you and your loved ones. Examine your lives and see how you may arrange them to enthrone the Divine Attributes I so desire you to embrace.

Determine to use your creative talents to construct the beautiful gardens that once graced Paradise. You shall realize the true value of things and become the citizens of Paradise once again.

What could be simpler than picking fruit from the garden and enjoying a daily swim, playing with your children and beloved friends, and singing joyful songs and praises to God? This is the simple life I would have you embrace again. This is the Real World I have created for you to enjoy.

The complicated, mechanistic society you have built is a blight upon the garden. I would have My Garden restored and all of My Children freed from the many futile labors you have created to pass your time so you may once again enjoy the simple life.

Eating from the garden will please our Maker.
The Banquet of Nature shall be our Feast.

Live Naturally

Oh, My Precious Children,

I would have you live naturally. Grow a garden, recycle your wastes, and protect your home from pollutants. This is the way of the future, and only those who do so will enjoy lives rich in happiness and health on this Earth. For this is the Natural Way which must return. All systems of this planet, which men have contrived, must be restored to natural, healthful living. The time of pollutants must end. The wages of sin are death, death to those who do not live according to the Laws of Nature and in harmony with My Divine Mandates.

You would do well to grow a garden to furnish your daily needs. Grow organic produce, including fruit and nut trees tended with care. These shall comprise the mainstay of your diet on Earth. This is how to live naturally, and it is My Law.

For you see, eating highly processed foods is injurious to your health. They are lacking in vitality and their natural essence is destroyed and tainted by chemicals used as preservatives, artificial flavors, additives, colorants, and mold retardants. These many unnatural products, which have found their way into the food of modern civilization, are toxic and responsible for many of the ailments suffered today. There has never been a time on this planet when so many insecticides, herbicides, chemicals and synthetic compounds have been used so widely and are so prevalent in all areas of life, especially in food growing, processing, and storage.

So be wise, My Darling Ones, get your hands in the soil and grow some beautiful, healthful plants of delicious varieties. Raise them organically using compost and natural fertilizers, which will restore the life to the land. You may prepare a finely ground mixture of pulverized rock, crushed to a fine powder-like consistency, that floats when sprinkled in the wind. Add this to your gardens and watch them grow.

Rock dust is the natural way to fertilize and remineralize the soil. Volcanoes create this rock dust and rely on the winds to spread it around the world. If each of you would spread rock dust on the agricultural lands and the global forests, the volcanoes would go dormant and sleep.

This I do require of those who would know Me fully and receive My Holy Spirit abundantly: Eat natural and healthy foods that are filled with life. Do abhor the use of chemically treated, synthetic, and overly processed foods, which devitalize the body and cause an unending array of diseases and every suffering imaginable.

Eating from the garden will please Your Maker. I would have you eat a meal comprised solely of vegetables, herbs, and fruits of the garden each day. I would have you fortify this meal with juice from carrots, celery, beets, and other vegetables. I would have you also add a sprinkling of seeds and nuts to your salads and fortify them with sprouts of many varieties. There is no need to use chemically manufactured, synthetic compounds to dress your salads. Try discovering the natural flavors, and when your palate has become accustomed to them you will relish the many different flavors I have created for you to enjoy.

Bring Me the bounty of your harvest for a celebration of the God Force within each growing thing. These foods create abundant health and nourish you for the many jobs you undertake to do My Will and live in harmony. This glorious feast should honor the Spirit behind all things; the Spirit I AM so abundantly providing you with each and every moment of your lives here on Earth.

A meal of fresh fruit in the morning upon rising is the very best way to stimulate your systems and give you quick vital energy to begin your day. This is most preferred over stimulants such as coffee and cigarettes, or eating dead or defiled foods such as cooked meats, eggs, or refined breads and flour products.

It is also wise for you to have one meal based on proteins. These proteins should consist of the natural varieties of nuts and seeds, legumes and grains, and beans and corn. Eat flour products, which are naturally processed, or sprouted before loaves are formed, such as the Essene "Bible bread" of old, which will prosper the body with vitality in great abundance. You may create ovens of glass and brick, which bake naturally in the sun at low temperatures. These highly wholesome, sprouted grains from organic wheat, barley, flax, rye, and other grains and seeds are available in your health food stores. Be sure your grains come from organically composted, naturally fertilized soils and are free of chemical mold retardants, radiation, chemical, or synthetic preservatives.

It is well that you consider that only life begets life and honor your bodies by keeping them free from the atrocities of malnutrition and suffering due to chemical synthetics. You must be accountable to fully research the foods you eat and make sure they are health-giving, or you will suffer needlessly.

Dear One, I would have you know that beneficial rays of light purify your blood naturally as you gaze upon the rising or setting sun.

Cleanse Yourself

Cherished Ones,

It is wise to regain your health and protect your families and your homes during these trying times of rampant pollution. To do so, endeavor to clean your homes with water, steam, and oxygen-based cleansers, such as hydrogen peroxide, rather than the many household cleansers that pollute the immune systems of the inhabitants of your home.

Do this for Me: take all of the chemicals that you have stored in your basements, garages, under your sinks in the kitchen, and in bathrooms and any storage cabinets containing cleaning solvents, paint thinners, and the like, and remove them from your home. Do not store them on the premises.

The next thing you can do to regain your health is to remove yourselves and your homes, if necessary, from areas that are plagued by pollution, whether it be in the soil, the air, or pollution carried along the waterways. To be really healthy, you need to be in a pollution-free environment.

It is wise to endeavor to replace the toxic load on your immune system with health-giving and rejuvenating oxygen compounds, such as hydrogen peroxide and ozone. Use these wonderful oxygen products to disinfect your drinking water and the water in which you bathe. Ozone is a natural antiseptic, antiviral, and anaerobic organism disinfectant, which will cleanse your homes of accumulated molds, mildew, and fungus. Ozone machines are available to eliminate these pollutants from the air within your household. Ozone destroys a variety of organisms growing in the dust that gathers within your precious homes. An ionizer machine can help eliminate the dust particles suspended in the air you breathe.

It is wise to go through your old bedding, mattresses, clothing, and other stored articles and discard those that you no longer use. These items can become breeding places for mold and mildew. Cleaning up your environment will play a major role in healing your bodies.

For your normal diet, partake of fresh greens daily and fresh ripe fruits. These will restore an immune system stressed by pollution and bring vitality to those in need. Eat neither fish, nor fowl, nor animal meat of any kind.

Jesus suggested that His patients eat grapes to restore their health and vitality. This was accomplished by the blessings of the fruit of the vine. Do eat grapes as your principle remedy in a mono-diet, which lasts for seven to ten days annually. Let the Angels of air, sunlight, and water caress your bodies each day. Focus on the Spirit behind all things, which gives you life. Honor that life by eating food that nourishes you and brings you better health.

Do press juice and drink it fresh each day. There are many juices that produce results for different ailments. Research these, and you will find many natural cures you may enjoy straight from the garden.

Just as you rid your homes of all the toxic chemicals and pollutants therein, also take the time and use your vital energy to cleanse your bodies of the toxins lingering there.

Internal cleansing can be accomplished in a variety of ways. There are herbal laxatives, purgatives, and colon irrigation treatments, which incorporate the use of water. This blessed Angel can help wash away years of encrustation within your colons. It is wise to use ozone to infuse the water with this health-giving, super oxygen-rich vitalizer that will also kill viruses within your colons and bloodstreams. So do use ozone liberally to treat your water and you will be blessed.

Go for a walk daily in nature and breathe in the clean air made fresh from the trees. This is vital. Do not stagnate by spending all your time dwelling within your homes, for they are the source of many of your health problems. You need fresh air, sunshine, and the blessings of nature to restore your health, in body, mind, and Spirit, so do not tarry, lingering indoors all the while.

Live in Peace

Dear Ones,

It is wise for you to make your homes in the pristine and beautiful areas available to you, rather than crowding yourselves into cities of strife and stress. I never intended for you to pave over the life-giving soil and live in small cubicles with stagnant air from air conditioners and heating systems.

Claim your birthright to enjoy life on earth, in nature, as I have intended you to do. Find a place where you may have a garden and raise your families in peace. There you may experience solitude and enjoy nature. I AM most happy when you take the time to be still and realize My Presence all around you.

Find Me in the living and blossoming plants, flowers, and trees, butterflies, birds, and bees, in the glades, meadows, and majestic mountains, and in the streams, lakes, rivers, and the wide blue ocean. Come and begin your lives anew in the beautiful places I have created for you to enjoy.

If you must live in cities, then do try to find as much peace as you can and bring the plants of the glades and forests into your home that they may bless you with fresh, clean air. There are many plants that grow well in the shade, and I encourage you to find them and bring them indoors.

There is much to do to rebuild this world of Mine, and I would have you all take an interest in preserving your beautiful planet by becoming involved in the many reconstruction projects to be initiated shortly. The reforestation of this vast planet with trees and plants will bring a source of food and fragrant flowers to the many hillsides and lands now occupied by cattle. Do find the time to volunteer to do whatever you can to help manifest My Glorious Kingdom here on Earth, and We shall create a garden more splendid than the Garden of Eden. We shall create Paradise on Earth.

Trust

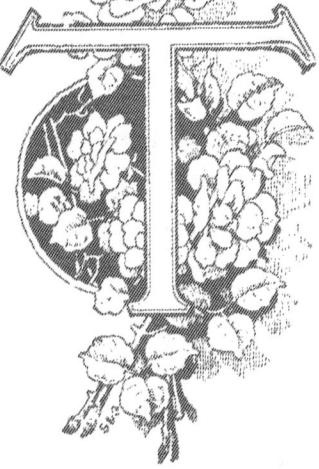

Dear Ones,

Trust is the foundation of Faith, and therefore, the most important element in any endeavor you pursue with your fellows or with Your Heavenly Father. Of all the Divine Graces I would choose you to adopt, please hold as sacred the Divine Attribute of Trust.

Trust is an attitude that reflects foresight and the ability to discern how far you can proceed with any blessed endeavor you undertake. It is most important for you to begin to find the time to Trust yourself by your steadfast determination to hold onto the Truth and proclaim it in your words. Truth may be ascertained by going within and deciphering the true meanings of beliefs that are held strongly. It is wise to question everything and delve into the heart of the matter, so that you may ascertain for yourself the Truth of all that is. Do not be misled or accept as Truth many of the concepts you have trusted to be true, for they are not.

Many people believe they do not have to contribute to the evolution of their Spirit Nature. They believe it is enough simply to be, but simply being will not bring them to Godhood. One must earnestly pursue Righteousness and obey Divine Directives, which bring the Attributes of Spirit into one's life. By actively pursuing these Supernal Goals and giving up the dross — relinquishing the lower animalistic nature and consciously elevating one's thoughts and mastering one's emotions — then one gains a measure of mastery that will eventually lead to the Divine State of Godhood.

This course must be actively pursued in order for the Supreme Goal to be reached. That is why I have given you Determination, Courage, and Faith, so you may choose Righteousness and exemplify it in your life by your own stalwart determination. In this way and no other shall you realize the Divine Goal of Godhood.

It is wise that you have endeavored to pursue this path of Divine Choosing, for as you choose to become Divine, you become a living example of Merciful Compassion that you demonstrate in your daily life to My Children everywhere. All the plants that grow and all the small creatures do cherish your Divine Attributes when you display them so kindly to My Beloved Ones.

Be Faithful to the Lofty Ideals recorded here, for I would have you make these Divine Graces a part of your personality, which is being made new as you give birth to the Divine Attitude that is changing your basic character. It is through character development that you embody these Heavenly Attributes. The Angels have brought them to Earth to Grace you all and inspire you to become who you really are inside.

Prayer

My Prayerful One,

Come to Me whenever you have a question or need a blessing of any kind. I will be happy to answer your every need.

Please address your prayers to the Holy Spirit who hears every word you speak and knows the motive of every heart. She will be your True Emissary for the Divine Answer you seek. The Holy Spirit is infinite and all-wise. She will bring every petition of the Soul to My Ears and help answer every question. It is wise to address this Blessed Being, My Holy Spirit, whenever you seek an answer to the ordinary questions of purely material needs and desires that may be fulfilled in this world.

As to the more perplexing spiritual questions pertaining to the life of each Soul, I would have you pray to My Paradise Son, whom Jesus personified in your dear world.

When your Soul fills with the Supernal* Joy of your Lord, and your Soul does sing My Divine Attributes, then pray to your Dear Father in Heaven and send forth your worshipful praise to Paradise.

Take all things that may be asked and bring them to the respective Deity who may best answer each question or longing of your Soul and endeavor to bring only your divine joy and gratitude to your Heavenly Father.

It is true that your Father in Heaven knows every need before you do, and I AM, therefore, endeavoring to provide you with all you shall ever need. It is a matter of faith for you to accept that your needs will be fulfilled before you even ask, and this is a great stepping-stone of Spirit. I would have you realize that, by faith, all of your needs can be met, even before they become needs. Do endeavor to relinquish the bonds of fear and come into the Light of Trust. There I can bring all of your desires to the table where the Feast of Your Beloved Father is awaiting your Divine Presence.

Addressing Your Prayers

Please Address:

1. The Holy Spirit for material needs and desires.

2. The Divine Son for spiritual questions regarding your Soul.

3. Your Heavenly Father for Worship, Divine Joy and Gratitude.

4. In addition, you also have a Spirit-Shard of the Great Heart-Crystal of God residing in your mind. Your personal Thought Adjuster is also known as a Father-Fragment. You may address all questions to your indwelling Father-Fragment to decipher God's Will in all potential choices you face.

Learn to listen to your Divine Intuition. My Spirit will help you whenever you ask.

The Holy Grail of Christ Consciousness

Drink of My Essence, the Blood of Christ. Eat of My Body that Christ ascended. Treasure this Covenant that the Lord has accepted. Break Bread for the Glory of God, The Heavenly Father, Who lives in the Perfect Reaches of the Heart. Blessed Be His Name: I AM. The Holy Spirit does Grace you with the Love which comes from on High. Take this Cup which holds the Life Blood of your Dear Creator and bring this Blessed Communion to the Father of All. Receive
the Power
of Christ
within
your
Soul.
Embrace
the Divine Nature
and become a Living Christ.

The Holy Sacrament of Christ

Dear One,

Listen to Me when I call to bring you home to the Heart of Love. My Most Cherished One, how far you have come in the race for the Treasures of Heaven. You are gracing this Beloved Realm with so very much. I have seen and heard and know all you do for Me. I AM with you this very moment, and I Bless your Soul as you partake of this Divine Covenant. I Will always Love you, My Cherished One. Align with My Divine Spirit as you bring forth the Divine Attributes I have instilled in your Soul.

You will bring forth the fruits that even now are blossoming within you. It is time to relinquish all of the dross that has ever encumbered you. Your erring thoughts and perceptions must dissolve so you may stand in My Light and deliver My Holy Nature unto the world, to your brothers and sisters.

So take the time to bring forth the Precious and Divine Nature with which I have endowed you, and you shall surely Shine forth the Divine Attributes of Being for all in your presence to plainly see. At every turn, look for Me and I will be here for you.

When you partake of the Holy Sacrament My Dear Son Jesus has offered you, you shall surely know what it is like to be a Christed One. You will bring forth the Divine Nature of Christ as this Special Treasure is imparted through your body into your Soul. The bread and wine is alive with My Divine Life Currents. The Sacred Covenant and Holy Sacrament of the Divine is yours to partake of and hold in every cell and in every thought, each and every moment of your splendid existence here on this Bountiful Earth.

There is so much I would like to say to you, My Beloved One, so very much I would like to shower upon you in these moments when you partake of the Divine Nectar I have given you. So make this day a Holy Day and endeavor to find Me and My Love for you within your precious Soul. For I AM here and I Love it when you come to Me, arms wide open, and give all you have for the Divine Purpose of establishing My Heavenly Kingdom in your heart and on this precious world.

Do this for Me at least once a week and you shall know Christhood as your own Power and Mantle of Glory. For I AM bestowing that upon you now, as you partake of the body and blood of My Dear Son, Jesus.

Be kind to all those you meet and consider that I AM surely the Silent Witness to every thought, word, and action you project in Divine Love to all your associates and brethren. I commend you on your emancipation from the dross and all you have relinquished so you may hold My Love within the Sacred Chalice of your Perfect Heart.

It is very wise for you to begin to see Me in everything around you. I AM with you when you behold My Beauty in nature. Therefore, see Me in everything, and you shall surely be Blessed in the days to come. This, do for Me, Beloved, and you shall surely see Heaven every time you look through your precious eyes to behold My Glorious Kingdom on Earth.

Bring Me your Sweetness

Dear One,

Do permeate the air and the world around you with sweetness and gentleness. Listen for My Voice, and hear the sweet rhapsody of Spirit nurturing your Soul with Unending Love. Know I Am here. Feel Me Glowing within each cell of your body. I AM the Wind softly caressing your cheek. I AM the Beautiful and Precious Feelings that well up within your heart when you contemplate the Divine Aspects of Being.

My Darling, when you find Me here within your heart, your heart will sing with a joy heretofore untold and unexpressed until that glorious moment when you discover We Are One.

So be kind to yourself, My Chosen One, and realize I AM here beside you, and inside you, and I will never leave you.

My Precious Darlings, I AM here to guide you safely along the path of right-choosing, to create the Gardens of the Lord, wherein you shall all blossom as My Precious, Divinely Fragrant Flowers. Your essence will bring the sweetness of Spirit to all you encounter, and the gentleness and peace of the Lord will dwell in your hearts and homes forevermore.

Manifesting Abundance

Dear Ones,

Those of you who seek to manifest abundance in your lives may do so to countless perfection. Begin by daily expressing the attitudes that manifest abundance: being thankful, grateful, and having trust, appreciation, and steadfast faith. These spiritual qualities bear fruit in the material world. Expressed sincerely, these attributes bring the grace to manifest abundance in your lives.

The power of positive thinking will help you attain your goal. You may master the art of mental prowess by practicing the expulsion of "fear" and "lack" from your mind whenever those negative thoughts drift into your consciousness.

There is another thing you can do to make abundance leap into your presence: ask for it. Make a list and pray for help, addressing your requests to My Holy Spirit. Meditate upon it often, focusing your attention upon the details of your desires.

Please do complete your list today and focus on what I may help you create. Bring Me into the picture, My Darling, to assist you in every way. This I will do most joyfully, for I AM the Power precipitating* all creation now. Repeat these words often: "I AM the power of precipitation acting now," and witness My Grace as the Universal Alchemy brings into existence all elements required for the creation of your desires.

You must focus your energy. Really concentrate on your intention, and I do promise amazing results which will open you to receive an unlimited supply of whatever you desire. Focus your attention upon your desired goal. Create it in your imagination. See yourself creating it from the ethers. Watch it appear as if by magic. Tell yourself you can and will accomplish this miracle and that you will use it to benefit all life on Earth. This will be easy for you to accomplish, for I have been opening you to receive My Blessings. Align your intent with My Will to create all for you.

My Perfect Love, I AM here to accomplish miracles. I AM filling the void with a Universe of Stars which is being born from the depths of space and appearing where there was nothing but My Intention to manifest a Glorious Creation. Therefore, give all to Me and your life will be enriched by Abundance.

Hope

ood Child,

I would like to comment upon the Attribute of Hope and how it may foster a growing realization of Faith in your life. Faith and Hope are closely related, Hope being the precursor of the Divine Attribute of Faith. It is wise, in all you say and do, always to hope for the best when you present your ideas and creative efforts to the world. Hope is an Attribute of Idealism and you may incorporate it in your life by adjusting your thoughts and feelings so that they are in tune with your divine ideals and hopeful accomplishments.

You may accomplish much in setting forth the perfect frequency of your desire, by clothing your desire in Hope. In the Perfect workings of Destiny, Hope brings the desire of your heart to the attention of the Divine Personalities surrounding your life's mission.

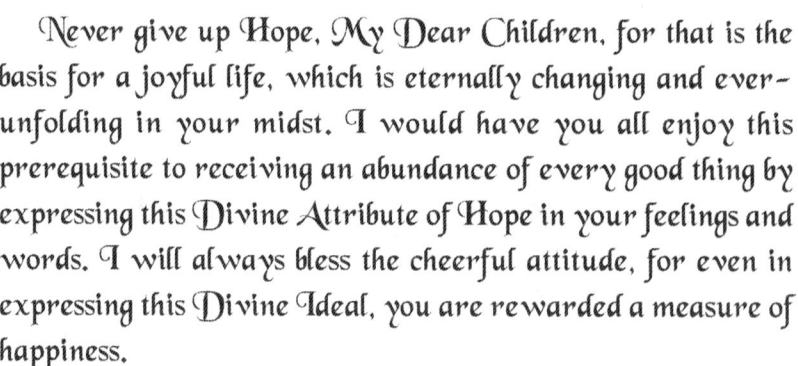

Hope is an especially valuable attitude to call forth, for indeed, Hope is a magnet that attracts abundance.

Never give up Hope, My Dear Children, for that is the basis for a joyful life, which is eternally changing and ever-unfolding in your midst. I would have you all enjoy this prerequisite to receiving an abundance of every good thing by expressing this Divine Attribute of Hope in your feelings and words. I will always bless the cheerful attitude, for even in expressing this Divine Ideal, you are rewarded a measure of happiness.

Hope often leads to reliance on Faith, which draws to the believer everything that is needed, often before the need is known by My Dear Ones who execute this Faithful Attribute.

Do bring Me your hopes and dreams so I may help you fulfill your Divine Potential and bring into being the beautiful creations which I AM inspiring you with, through My Holy Spirit and the Divine Inspiration of My Blessed Angels.

A note from the author

I would like to tell you just a little bit about my life, so you can know who is bringing forth God's Words in His Own Name. For most of my life, I thought of myself as separate from God. And although I loved Him very much and honored Him, I did not understand where He was. Even though Jesus said, "The kingdom of God is within you," still, I did not realize it. I thought that God lived high off in His heavenly clouds looking down over me. It did not occur to me that He was here within me all the time.

When I was sixteen years of age, I experienced death. I must have been poisoned, because I became so violently ill that I did not have the strength to stand or walk. My sister carried me up the stairs and laid me in my bed. I wretched and dry heaved until I became so weak I couldn't move at all. The pain and sickness were unbearable. And then, everything went black. I saw a spotlight focused on the back of a man's head. Slowly he turned around and I was horrified to see that it was the Devil, and he was laughing at me.

I prayed for Lord Jesus to help me. Suddenly, it seemed as if I were at the bottom of the ocean with a whirlpool sucking me down. I couldn't breathe. I swam, struggling against the current with all my might. It took every ounce of strength I possessed. As I rose, I noticed that the water got stiller towards the top and easier to ascend. Above me, I could see the surface. I swam on until at last, I broke through where I could breathe.

To my astonishment, I kept ascending right up through the peaking waves. I looked down, and in complete surprise, saw what I had believed to be the ocean was the atmosphere of Earth. I had risen above it into space. I could see the whole world below me. It was infinitely beautiful to behold. I looked towards the sun and it was magnificent, so brilliant! Then I saw, in the far distance, two beautiful Angels shining brighter than the sun. They were flying towards me. A thrill of joy went through me as I thought, "They are going to take me to God." How beautiful they looked. They were the most beautiful beings I had ever seen, and yet, I didn't even have eyes to see. I didn't have a body at all, just a point of consciousness that could behold all the wonder and beauty around me.

When I started out towards them, I heard a Great Voice within me saying, "Wait there. You do not understand how it is." The Voice was kind, compassionate, infinitely loving, neither male nor female, pure, all-powerful, yet gentle... a Voice that seemed to come from the heart of eternity.

As the Angels came closer they spoke, and their words rang all around me and through me. "It is your Father's will," they said, "that you return to Earth. There is something of utmost importance that must be done during your lifetime, something that only you can do." I thought to myself, "Who, me? What could I possibly do that could make a difference?" And then it dawned on me, "Oh, they must have a case of mistaken identity. They have confused me with someone else, someone important."

The Angels said, "Do you want to do your Fathers will?" I felt disappointed, because I really wanted to be with God more than anything. Yet, there was no way to argue with a question like that. "Yes," I thought. "I do want to do my Father's will." And, as I resigned myself to His will, I suddenly sped through the atmosphere until I came to a stop, hovering just above my house.

I had super vision and super hearing! I saw my friend asleep in his bed through the rooftop of his house, three houses away. I could hear his dog breathing. In awe, I began to look around. Then I heard the Angles again; "Do you want to do your Father's will?

As I thought, "Yes," I descended through my rooftop, hovering near the ceiling above my dead body. Surprisingly, I was repulsed by it. Although I had enjoyed my life, I had no desire to go back into that cold lump of flesh. Then, I heard the Angels asking me again, "Do you want to do your Father's will?" And as I thought, "Yes," I suddenly flew into my body. I was stuck, and it felt as if I weighed a thousand pounds, considering a few moments earlier I had the freedom of weightlessness. I was tired, so very tired, but I thanked Jesus because the sickness was gone and I was safe.

What I had been brought back to Earth for, my mission, was to bring God's Words to you now, so you may feel the direct personal experience of His Divine Love. It is God's Will that people everywhere receive the benefit of His Divine Guidance, so everyone can experience the peace, the blessed abundance, and absolute joy of Heaven on Earth now.

I focused on God a lot through my life, and He has spoken to me occasionally, always with miraculous consequences. My life was spared on numerous occasions, from horrific car crashes to attempted murder. By listening to God's Guidance, I have overcome many seeming tragedies and recovered from crippling connective tissue disease. When doctors gave me no hope of recovery from an autoimmune disease that landed me in a wheelchair, I was led by God's Unerring Guidance to a remarkable recovery. I have endured many broken bones, including a broken back, and all these have healed completely. When I was healing, I had more time to focus on improving my spiritual life, so I made God my full-time job.

In 1991 I focused on Him five to seven hours each day for nine months. Each morning I hiked up a remote sea cliff an hour before dawn. There I sat in God-Contemplation* for an hour before sunrise. Every day I felt His Divine Love and experienced ultimate peace. I reached the breathless state and experienced cosmic consciousness. God always opened my eyes the exact moment the sun began to rise, so I could behold His Light. Dolphins gathered by the hundreds in the sea below me.

Motionless, they floated, their dorsal fins rising above the surface of the water. Then, when I rose and stretched forth my hands to bless them, they would all jump at once, spinning with glee. Beyond them, families of great Humpback whales gathered, and closer in to the shore, ancient sea turtles clustered together below me. Above me, giant albatross' circled overhead, while my horse and little dog stood at attention before me. They all lined up for my blessing, for they loved receiving the gift of God's Pure Energy. I spoke aloud, blessing the creatures of the air, the land, and the sea. Then my blessing also reached out to you, flowing all around the world, gracing every person and all life everywhere.

Earlier, in 1981, Jesus had come to me in Spirit. He said, "I want to come through you." Thinking that He wanted to be born into the world again, I got pregnant that very month. I gave birth to a son, whom I called Jesse Kuhio Kalani (which means, God's gracious gift, a prince of Heaven). Jesse is, indeed, heaven sent. He is so filled with nurturing love and helpful wisdom that at Hana grade school, his class made up a special award, to honor him for being the most caring and sharing child in his school. But, ten years later, in 1991, when I was blessing all the world, Jesus came to me again, exactly as He had in the past. Again He said, "I want to come through you." Confused, I said, "I gave birth to Jesse so you could walk the earth again." Then Jesus said with extra emphasis on the last word this time, "I want to come through <u>YOU</u>."

When God asked me to be His emissary, I was worried that I wasn't good enough, or pious enough, or serious enough. I was always kidding around, so I thought that I'd better change my demeanor. Then He told me not to change a thing. He said, "Be light and joyful. Your laughter is especially loved by Me, and the Angels adore it." He said He loved me just the way I was and that when anything needed to be changed in me, He would make the changes.

In 1978, I asked God to take care of my financial needs so that I could work for Him full time, and He has provided for me in many surprising ways. God has also given me the ability to heal others, from migraine headaches to depression. He asked me to write about the miracles He brought into my life during Our Adventures Together, which is the subject of my forthcoming autobiography. Working for God through the years, I have written two screenplays and have compiled manuscripts for fifteen books thus far. Writing was hard for me, for I had to overcome both dyslexia and being an atrocious speller.

When I took the screenplay I had written for God to Hollywood, I met Gene Roddenberry, who offered me the opportunity to have a starring role, as a very spiritual, celibate alien in his first movie, "Star Trek, the Motion Picture." But, following God's Guidance, I turned him down, as well as an opportunity to star in the screenplay I had written. Saying no to these opportunities was the hardest test for me; but God had a greater career planned for me: a life devoted only to Him, far away from the distractions of the fast-paced, worldly, city life, where I could become divine by focusing my attention on God alone. He showed me a vision of a beautiful paradise, a pristine beach where the sun rose from the sea with a hillside pasture for my horse, SunDancer. So I moved to Kauai and after some searching, found the promised land.

In 1996, God asked me to record His Words for the new millennium verbatim. He asked me to bring a little hand held recorder when I came to commune with Him, rather than later trying to remember what I thought I had heard Him say. God also asked me to change my name to I AM. It was challenging, because I felt people would scrutinize me, or think I was crazy, or judge me as being egotistical for claiming I was God. Oh, how I wished He had asked me to build an ark instead... (not that I could have!) But now, I am happy that I did change my name and I know He's happy too, because every time I meet someone in His Name, I AM, the conversation always leads straight to God.

I AM is God, because the Great I AM is alive and conscious in everything, as everything. Every one of us is divinely blessed to be part of God's unfolding miracle of love and life. I feel so reverent to know that I am part of God, that His very Spirit is at the core of my being, that He talks to me, and guides me, and gives me His Divine Love. Now He wants to do that for you too.

People often ask me how I hear God. When I was younger, talking to God was like a one-way telephone conversation. I did all the talking and then hung up with a reverent "Amen." One day, I was inspired to listen. I decided to still my thoughts. It is impossible to think our own thoughts and hear God's Thoughts at the same time, because He will never intrude upon our thoughts. And so, I had to really focus on listening and not let any thoughts come to mind. It was hard at first. Sometimes He would only give me one word and I would have to wait for ten minutes to get the next one. And then, when I got a word wrong, one I thought He was going to say, or a thought came to mind getting in the way, He would stop. Then I would have to go back and see where I had gotten it wrong and begin again. He was very careful not to let me get any words wrong.

At our core, every one of us refers to ourselves as I am, though usually in the context of "I am hungry," or "I am full." God created us in His Image and His Divine Spirit lives in us, as us. When we seek His Inner Guidance and choose to do His Will, we become godly. By contemplating God's Divine Nature and feeling Divine Love, we eventually become divine personalities who identify with God's Holy Spirit, rather than thinking what we have been taught to believe, which is that we are ego based identities, unworthy of and separate from God.

When we experience a divine merger with God's Indwelling Spirit, we are elevated to the joyous throne of Heaven within. There, we celebrate a Divine Marriage of Sacred Spirit, and become Temples of the Most High Living God!

I have aligned my will with His Will, and my soul is filled with His Holy Spirit. I realize that I AM God's Living Temple. I have invited Him to speak up whenever He likes. Now, He wants to speak through me, to everyone on Earth.

At the burning bush, when God asked Moses to free His enslaved people, Moses asked God, "Who shall I say has sent me?" God replied, "I AM." Moses didn't understand, so God repeated, "I AM that I AM." But God could not get through the rigid constructs of Moses' ingrained beliefs. Moses could only conceive of God as Jehovah: angry, jealous, and wrathful. He was, to Moses, the God of the fiery volcano, who vented while Moses delivered the Ten Commandments to the Hebrews. That is the reason there are so many conflicting views of God's nature within Biblical scriptures. Jesus knew Moses' interpretation of God's nature was incorrect, so He taught that the One True God, whose name is I AM, is our loving Heavenly Father who resides in the Heaven within our hearts. Jesus said, "The Kingdom of God is within you."

Jesus realized God's presence within Himself and received God's Divine Love and Guidance directly. He spoke God's thoughts, proclaiming, "I AM the light of the world." He tried to explain to people, saying, "These things I tell you, I say not of myself. It is the Father within me that doeth the works." But, unless people have had a firsthand experience of God within themselves, it is a very hard concept to understand, especially when they have been taught to believe that God is a mighty fearful Deity that lives somewhere else. Believing it was heresy and blasphemy to profess union with God, many people thought Jesus was egotistically speaking about himself, and so, misunderstood His teachings and condemned Him. Jesus said that we are all sons and daughters of God. Yet after His death, people who didn't really understand what Jesus was trying to say wrote the Bible. Consequently, they referred to "God's chosen people" as being the Hebrews exclusively. In fact, all people are God's people and for those who are enslaved, God always does His best to inspire someone to set them free.

God wants each and every one of us to have an intimate love-relationship with Him. It is possible for you also to merge with Him and develop your power to heal yourself and others. Jesus said, "These things and greater things shall ye do also." Let us prove Him right by creating Heaven on Earth now in this new millennium, for "God's Kingdom will come, when His Will is done, on Earth as it is in Heaven."

Heaven on Earth

GOD's Words for the New Millennium
Volume II

Heaven on Earth

God's Word Definitions

God's Preface for Heaven on Earth

* endeavor – a campaign of earnest, conscientious, and concerted effort and purposeful industrious activity: the glorious enterprise of creating Heaven on Earth.

The New Dispensation

* indwells – residing within you, a Divine Inner Spirit is leading you to Godliness
* Divining – to make divine
* Darling – a dearly beloved person
* apprised – to become informed about
* Nebadon – name of the universe containing Earth

Introduction by Lord Jesus

* abide – to dwell or sojourn
* supernal – heavenly, celestial
* dross – impurity, worthless trivial waste including: the animalistic nature of the beast, sin, encumbered guilt, suffering, and corruption caused by erring beliefs, fear, negative or destructive thoughts, words, and deeds, egotistical control dramas and emotional baggage, greed, the dark side of man
* emancipation – to become free from bondage

The Divine Plan for Earth

* myriads – innumerable aspects or elements
* decimation – to destroy a large part of
* propagate – to cause animals and other organisms to breed or multiply, transmitting desirable characteristics from one generation to the next.
* foresight – forethought that requires planning to determine the outcome of the future based on current actions undertaken
* meticulous – careful consideration of details
* adjures – to urge or advise earnestly
* kilter – good condition or order
* wanton – irresponsible, reckless, without regard, lunatic
* exponentially – ever increasing rate of change

Grace

* formidable – awesome, influential, remarkable
* atoning – to make amends by restoring or offering restitution
* natural cycles – the laws of Nature which produce abundant diversified life on Earth

Heaven on Earth

* theocratical – Government by God: the constitution or polity of a country in which God is regarded as the sole sovereign and the laws of the realm are seen as divine commands

* monarchy - a government that is ruled by a man or woman sovereign, such as a king who reigns over a state or territory, usually for life and by hereditary right
* imperial - ruling over extensive territories or over colonies or dependencies: *imperial nations*
* monotheistic - the belief in one God
* altruistic - unselfish concern for the welfare of others;
* autarchic - from Greek *autarkhos*, self-governing ruler
* imperialistic - the policy of extending a nation's authority by territorial acquisition or by the establishment of economic and political hegemony over other nations
* democratic - believing in or practicing social equality
* equity - the state, quality, or ideal of being just, impartial, and fair. Justice applied in circumstances covered by law yet influenced by principles of ethics and fairness
* monistic - God's new interpretation of doctrine that there is one trinitized God who lives within all things as all things, and that humanity's true identity is the beneficent Godly Spirit that lives within the individual personality. This enlightened perspective of unity with God, which leads to divine character perfection, is attained by the sacred marriage of the Soul and Divine Spirit, unifying God within the individual, thus eliminating one's association with the separate identity of ego-self which is so prone to being destructive, and is the cause of misery, injustice, greed, and inequity.

* theocracy – the divine spiritual government of God (Heaven) within one's own heart that results from the Ascension in consciousness one progressively experiences when one becomes unified with God as their Divine Self. Also, Heaven on Earth, as people create Divine Laws to govern all peoples, animals, and nature beneficially.

Restoring Paradise on Earth

* expropriation – to immorally transfer (another's property) to oneself; rip off
* StarPower – God has inspired His Emissary, I AM, with a clean energy invention for a Global Solar Utility Company to provide everyone with safe, clean electrical power, fresh pure water and rich vegetable protein; the basic necessities of life for all. Utilizing StarPower and reforesting the planet will result in resurrecting Paradise and lay the foundation of the Kingdom of Heaven on Earth.

Divine Justice

* inaugural – to cause to begin, especially officially or formally
* commencement – a beginning or start
* adjudication – judicial settlement
* Sovereign – one that exercises supreme, permanent authority
* bent – determined to take a course of action

* justify – To make one just as God frees a human being of the guilt and penalty attached to grievous sin
* vindicated – to set free; protected from attack
* indemnify – redeem, reforest, replant, reclaim
* stave off – to keep or hold off; repel

Protect the Meek

* evaluate – to make a judgment of worth and set a value on
* disparage – put down, not do justice to
* sequestered – to set apart, separate
* insolent – disrespectful

Judgments

* levy – to impose or inflict

Kindness

* Hearken – Listen
* altruism – the practice of unselfish concern for the welfare of others
* philanthropy – giving money and voluntary work for love of humanity

Mercy

* adjudication – to pass judgment

* relish – to take pleasure in; enjoy
* redeemer – save from a state of sinfulness and its consequences

My Divine Law

* abomination – to dislike greatly, repulsive, detestable
* ennoble – to elevate in degree, excellence or respect; exalt

Your Daily Bread

* abjure – renounce

Guardians of Destiny

* ferrocement – thin cement slabs reinforced with steel mesh
* StarPower Energy Utility Company – God inspired, safe, clean electrical energy supplier
* conveyance – endowment: free power to everyone on Earth

Prayer

* Supernal – celestial, heavenly, being or coming from on high

Manifesting Abundance

* precipitating – Just as raindrops precipitate into form from moisture in the air that condences into a liquid form, so also, God creates by reforming the ethers or elements into matter, causing materialization to happen suddenly.

In this 21st Century update, GOD's Divine Plan to create **Heaven on Earth now** is revealed for all humanity. Feel a direct personal experience of GOD's Divine Love as you read these Holy Books for All the Ages.

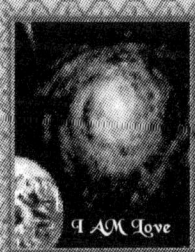   

Profits from the sales of these books will help create Heaven on Earth.

Enjoy Beautifully Illustrated, Inspiring Messages in full color & b&w Books, Audio Cassettes, Videos, e-books, and on CD Rom.

Join the Movement to Create
Heaven on Earth
IAMLOVE.TV

Heaven on Earth
Order Form

Phone orders Toll Free: 1-800-795-3069
E-mail: GODSWORDS@IAMLOVE.TV
Postal orders: Heaven on Earth
P.O. Box 398
Hanalei, Hawaii 96714

Rich with Angelic art, each book contains 200+ pages of beautifully illustrated, inspiring messages from Heaven. Quality paperbacks, signed by author...$19.95 each. Beautiful hard cover, full color, limited, signed, collectors edition ... $59.95 each.

Please send me the following books shown on the other side:
_____
_____

☐ Please send God's Heaven on Earth newsletter to me **FREE.**
☐ I have enclosed a question for God or my prayer request.

Company name:_____
Name:_____
Address:_____
City, state, zip:_____
Telephone: (____)_____ e-mail:_____

US Shipping; $4.00 for the first book and $2.00 each additional book.
International Shipping: $8 for the first book and $4 for each additional book.
Please make check made payable to: Heaven on Earth
Credit cards: ☐ VISA ☐ MC ☐ Optima ☐ Discover ☐ AMEX
Card Number:_____
Name on card:_____ Exp. date:____/____

Be an Earth Angel and join God's A-Team of Volunteers who create Heaven on Earth.

You can participate in Paradise reconstruction and in the enlightenment of humanity. God has given us a beautiful planet and the directive to restore paradise now. If you have time, a talent, or resources you would like to contribute, please let us know how you can help God achieve His Divine Plan to create Heaven on Earth now.

Projects are currently underway for:

Publishing God's ongoing transcripts. Calling all Angels to help finance the publishing of God's Words in order to make mass distribution and donations of books, audio tapes, and CD-ROMs possible.

Artists: Angel Art representing all nationalities sought to decorate God's Words.

Linguists sought to help translate God's Words into every language.

Centers are required worldwide to organize God's A-Team for the global reconstruction of Paradise. God's Children of all faiths are welcome. Perhaps your church, mosque, synagogue, temple, club, or organization would like to join this multi-denominational movement to create Heaven on Earth.

TV and radio shows and advertisements can spread the good word. Publicity in magazines, newspapers, and on the internet is essential.

Heaven on Earth - My Kingdom Come! God's TV ministry will also convene in cyberspace on a chat channel on Saturdays. Please join us and share your practical ideas for creating Heaven on Earth, for you and those around you.

One tree can make a difference for 200 years. Earth Angels like you can start fruit or nut trees that will help end world hunger. To find out about these projects and more log on to:

www.IAMLOVE.TV

www.ingramcontent.com/pod-product-compliance
Lightning Source LLC
Chambersburg PA
CBHW081834170426
43199CB00017B/2724